C000064578

POCKET IMAGES

Clay Cross Revisited

Albert Heath, photographer and draper, took this portrait in his
Thanet Street Studios, *c.*1910. The photograph depicts Bill Marshall,
trainer, and an unknown player. An early reference to football being
played in Clay Cross appears in the *Derbyshire Courier* in January 1874,
when the local team played against Chesterfield. 'This match played at
Chesterfield on Monday, ended in an easy victory for Chesterfield. The
Clay Cross Club was only formed last year (1873) so there was some
excuse for their defeat, although the Chesterfield team was not a strong
one. The Chesterfield players obtained 8 goals to their opponents' 0.
The players for Clay Cross were: T. King (captain), C.T. Murray, G.
Dore, G. Steene. J. Linacare. B. Brimlow, E. Bonsall, J.H. Unwin, J.
Walters, W. Lowe, T. Wilson and T. Millington. Chesterfield players
were: E. Francis (captain), Downey, E. Holehouse, G.E. Whomersley, T.
Riggot, J. Fletcher, J.H. Shaw, Walmesley, Roper, Smith, and Nail.'

POCKET IMAGES

Clay Cross Revisited

Cliff Williams

NONSUCH

In 1844, the Clay Cross Company (CXC), had the distinction of being the first 'inland' company to send coal direct to London by rail, via the London and Birmingham Line. To celebrate the occasion, 'a mass of coal 13ft long, 3ft 9ins broad by 2ft thick was taken out of the Blackshale Pit at Clay Cross. Had time allowed, a mass twice that size might have been obtained from the pit. It was dispatched entire by train.'

First published 2000
This new pocket edition 2007
Images unchanged from first edition

Nonsuch Publishing Limited
Cirencester Road, Chalford,
Stroud, Gloucestershire, GL6 8PE
www.nonsuch-publishing.com

Nonsuch Publishing is an imprint of NPI Media Group

British Library Cataloguing in Publication Data.
A catalogue record for this book is available from the British Library.

ISBN 978-1-84588-404-8

Typesetting and origination by Nonsuch Publishing Limited
Printed in Great Britain by Oaklands Book Services Limited

Contents

Acknowledgments

First of all many thanks to Nobby Clark for allowing me to read through his unpublished manuscript on local football, which he is meticulously compiling. This has helped me considerably with the chapter on the town's football teams. Unfortunately, due to the priorities in selection and the limitations of the publication, the chapter on football has been much reduced, but several other footballing photographs may appear in another volume in the near future. Once again many thanks to Alan Harris for his help and continuing support with this pictorial project, and the Biwater Company for access to the archives which has contributed much to all three volumes. At the time of writing, however, and the pending take-over of the Biwater Company, there is much concern by local historians and workers about what might happen to the extensive company archive that they are currently custodians of, but more importantly what might happen to several hundred jobs, the main stay of the local economy!

My gratitude and thanks to the North Wingfield History Group for their continued support during the time it has taken to prepare this volume; Peter Wilson for some excellent photographs taken during the mid-1960s and early 1970s, which have certainly enhanced this volume and particularly those of the Whitwalks and Clay Cross Station; Alan Allsop for material on Chistmas Hayes, the Clay Cross Station Master; Bob Gratton and Stuart Band for Ashover Light Railway information; Dorothy Tilley for some excellent school photographs; Chesterfield and County Library, Local Studies and County Archive Staff who have been most helpful and supportive during my research on all three volumes, and Nonsuch Publishers for deciding to publish this third volume in their *Pocket Images* Series, which demonstrates the popularity and success of the previous two volumes.

Sincere thanks to all those people who have in some small way supplied either a photograph or just a snippet of information: George (Nudder) Findley, Billy Tooley, Margaret North, Bill Lomas, Ernie Whitworth, Dorothy Tilley, Graham Skinner, Harold Maycock, Sid Kilpin, Via Slater, Christine Morgan, Ronnie Lunn, Joe Foster, Mick Brady, Mick Holmes, John Woodhouse, Chuck Hawkins, Joe Stevens, Alice Hallowes, Arthur Haslam, Susan Holmes, Cliff Cresswell, Louie and John Rees, Mrs M. Limb, Stuart Band, Jim Leverett and the late Richard Micheal Hale for his photographic expertise. A mega thanks must also go to the late Albert Heath, professional photographer, whose prolific production has made an enormous contribution to this pictorial archive project and I would like to dedicate this project to his memory. Also to Frank Webster for his good company and 'tap room' snippets about our town's recent past which have been illuminating and informative. Once again the *Derbyshire Times*, *Derbyshire Courier*, *Derby Mercury* and *Clay Cross Chronicle* have all been invaluable, so many thanks to their past and present editors, journalists, photographers and readers.

Finally many thanks to my wife Anne for her patience and good humour, my two daughters, Anne Marie and Rachel, and my granddaughter Olivia for not playing shop with my computer discs and practising Karaoke during the time I've been working on this project. My sincere apologies to any one that I might have excluded in these acknowledgements.

Introduction

The first volume *Clay Cross and the Clay Cross Company*, was principally about the company's industrial activities that have been so important to the local and north-east Derbyshire economy for some 160 years. This collection has brought together some rare and evocative images of coal-mining, captured by photographer Albert Heath just after the turn of the twentieth century, and produced as a set of postcards to celebrate the winning of a gold medal for the company's coal products at the Franco British Exhibition in London, 1908. Other photographs and postcards recorded show various scenes in the foundry, coke ovens, pipe bank, farms etc, along with some stunning images of the quarries and lime kilns at Crich and Ambergate. The company's collieries that once dominated the local landscape at Clay Cross, Morton, Danesmoor and Wingerworth, have now been levelled into obscurity, but not before they were recorded for posterity in written and photographic evidence. The company's paternal organizations and institutions such as schools, housing and chapels, which helped to recruit, retain and mould a compliant and sober workforce, have also been well documented.

The second volume continued with a small industrial chapter, but with a predominant emphasis on the town's urbanization, which almost depicts a nineteenth-century Clay Cross with its comprehensive street scenes and service industry. Another focus of attention was the variety of community activities including carnivals, Whitwalks, and Coronation celebrations. This aspect of the town has been further developed in this third volume, and there are some fascinating pictures that are certain to rekindle some nostalgia and gossip.

The third volume, like the previous two, does not profess to be a history of the town or neighbourhood, but simply a visual dimension to that understanding and provisional process called history. Once again, Albert Heath, the town's photographer, has contributed much to this volume. There is an emphasis on the sporting and recreational activities of the town with an excellent selection of Heath's football photographs, taken at the turn of the twentieth century. Organized football appears to have commenced in the town during the 1870s boom period, and together with the development of the High Flat as a cricket ground, this promoted and encouraged a diversion from 'John Barleycorn' and trade unionism. Indeed, the company's continuing paternal interventions can be discerned throughout this volume and the Jackson's contributions are most evident.

The community chapter shows an excellent selection of the 1960s Whitwalks, showing buildings which were demolished during the towns' massive rebuilding programme, initiated by Dennis Skinner and his comrades. They disposed of hundreds of houses that were considered unfit for human habitation, a legacy of the Spivs and Speculator developments of the nineteenth century. The photographs of the 1960s will generate much interest as many inhabitants will recognise themselves participating in the Whitwalk or watching the procession. The town's Working Men's clubs are well represented, together with the Danesmoor Miners Welfare and their associated recreational interests. Darts and dominoes continue to play an important role in local pub activities, both socially and financially. The Sheldon Darts Cup, inaugurated in 1940, is still competed for and will be celebrating its sixtieth anniversary this year.

The transport section in this volume includes Joseph Sutton, a local carrier, who plied between Clay Cross, Chesterfield and Mansfield. Photographs and documents of the local toll gates and information on the Turnpike Trusts at Clay Cross, Smithymoor, and Badger Lane, reveal a little about the local transport history prior to the arrival of the railways. There are some superb photographs of the Clay Cross railway station, particularly of its closure in December 1966. There are also some images of the local Wagon Works at Hepthorn Lane, and the Stretton Station depicts an idyllic rural railway setting with images of the Ashover Light Railway which concludes this chapter.

The uniform chapter assembles some superb images of the Clay Cross Volunteers which was established in 1860. Their successors, the Territorials (formed in 1908), together with the Cyclist Company, Regimental Band and Mascot are all assembled for inspection. Also depicted in this chapter are the Guides, Scouts, Boys Brigade and fire brigade, and a rare photograph of the town's First World War Trophy captured by the 6th Battalion at Canal Du Nord.

The chapter on the company, together with the references in the two previous volumes, completes a comprehensive visual documentation of the town's industry with some rare views of the pig beds, blast furnaces, the Big Wall and stocking ground. The chapter concludes with some interesting photos on the removal of the Big Tip which has heaped up 125 years of colliery and foundry spoils and is about to be further flattened with the town's impending developments.

The final chapter shows some unique photos of the 1922, 1931 and 1936 Parliamentary elections and concludes with the Badge of Office being disposed of, and a determined Dennis Skinner early in his political career. Images of the Rent Struggle against the so-called Tory Fair Rent Act which put Clay Cross on the map will have to wait for the next volume!

Once again, deadlines, time restraints, elusive facts, memory lapses and the anonymity of so many people depicted in this volume are bound to make a production of this nature inadequate and incomplete! However, readers will once again be able to remove some of the anonymity by putting names to a few faces and can perhaps elaborate on a few events and functions, particularly those images depicted in the 1960s. I feel sure that this volume will be eagerly received and will contribute a little more to the towns' visual archive and will give some context and background to family historians whose ancestors worked, played and lived in Clay Cross.

Cliff Williams
June 2000

One
Community

In March 1922, the Co-op decided to set back the front of their property and 'throw it into the street if the council paid them £300'. In January 1924, the Urban District Council asked the National West Provicianal Bank to do the same to improve the road access. The first bank in the town was established by the CXC who established a Working Men's Saving Club in 1846 and incorporated a Female Savings Club in 1851. A Penny Bank commenced in the town as early as April 1866 and 'This valuable institution is continuing its upwards progress. It has been in operation for about 12 months and numbers 165 depositors. Deposited last Saturday evening £6 0s 4d; withdrawls 9s 6d and total deposits £95'. On the first of April, 1876, it was reported that the North Derbyshire and Chesterfield Banking Company opened a branch in Clay Cross, in the committee rooms of the Co-op. During this boom period The Sheffield Banking Company also opened a branch on the High Street.

High Street, c.1900, looking south with the Star Hotel to the right. On the left of the photograph, at the corner of Eyre Street is Hilton's Booteries who were advertising in the *Clay Cross Chronicle* in January 1910: 'Judge us by the value we give in Boots and Shoes. No better value on earth. Hilton's Booteries High Street Clay Cross corner of Eyre Street. Also in 100 other towns'.

Another view of the High Street, showing the Crown Pub which was the registered office of the Engine Mens and Firemens Union, established on 22 February 1892. In March 1903, Harry Claytor succeeded Mr Wood as the landlord of the Crown and he remained as such until his death in February 1908. Harry served twenty-one years with the 2nd Clay Cross Battalion Volunteers and was awarded the long service medal, attaining the rank of Sergeant. He was appointed under-manager of No. 4 Pit in 1893, a post which he held for ten years.

Lower High Street, c.1905, showing a much narrower turn into Market Street just after the Elm Tree Pub. On the left is Saunderson's shop, No. 1 Victoria Buildings, with an Ingersol Watch hung outside. An advertisement in 1910 records the shop as an old hairdressing salon and umbrella makers. John Saunderson was the proprietor and successor to the late William Saunderson who had established his business in Clay Cross as early as 1840. On the left is Bell's Stores, 'The Modern Cash Grocer' with its large metal sign prominent on the building.

The Bestwood Working Men's Club committee, c.1912. The first attempt to establish a club in Thanet Street failed in February 1911. According to the local press, Clay Cross Working Men's Club and Institute was 'struck off the register' for breaching the licensing laws when the promoters took over the Dusty Miller pub which was closed down under the Compensation Act and could not be used for at least twelve months.

Councillor Bill Lander drawing a pint of beer in the Bestwood Working Men's Club, December 1967, to celebrate £21,000 worth of improvements. From small beginnings, the club extended its premises in 1926 with the addition of a concert hall and further improvements were made in 1947 and 1959. In 1967, Don Morris was president of the club, Jack Porter the secretary, and Doug Hollyoak entertainments manager. Audrey Graham was top of the bill with Ken Johnson comedian and Cliff Renshaw singer.

The Danesmoor Miners' Welfare was opened in September 1925. The money to run the scheme was obtained by putting a penny per ton on the output of coal at each colliery, and every man working for the company was encouraged to contribute a penny per week. The scheme included all employees of the company and Clay Cross residents could become members of the Welfare scheme by contributing 4s 4d per annum.

Above: Mr H. Parkin, the areas NUM general secretary, supported by Dennis Skinner, cuts the tape to open the extension at the Clay Cross and Danesmoor Miners Welfare, on 13 February 1968. This extension increased the floor area by a third at a cost of £4,000. At this date the membership was around 1,300, and Mr H. Tomlinson was general secretary.

Below: After seventy years as a local Methodist preacher, Mr James Simms decided to retire on his ninetieth birthday: 'I've absolutely no regrets at having given so much time to the church, but I'm beginning to feel a little out of place. Mind you I shall preach again if I'm needed'. From left to right: G.H. Tuckley, Mrs E. Fearn, Mrs Bowns, -?-, Mr J. Simms, Revd E. Bower, Mr J. Clewlow, Mr V. Tuckley. Jim's dad was killed in the Parkhouse Pit explosion in November 1882.

Clay Cross Works 18th Show and Gala, 25 August 1967. This show resulted in 408 entries in the flower and vegetable sections. Harold Barlow won the New Foundry Cup for most points in this combined section. The Bridget Jackson Cup for the domestic section was won by Mrs Holmes, and George Eyre won the 'H' Welfare Cup for best flowers. John Bunting won the Jackson Cup for photography and the cricket knockout was won by the pattern shops workers' team, and the tug of war by the machine shop workers' team.

Clay Cross Hall garden party, 1 July 1967, opened by Joan and Peggy Jackson, daughters of the late Brig. Jackson, for the benefit of the Residents Amenities Fund. Mrs Peggy Hawkins, second from left and Mrs E. Hawkins, third from left, are supervising the jumble stall. A competition for guessing the weight of a 210lb lump of coal was won by Miss M. Parsons of Chesterfield. At one time the CXC considered that 120lbs made a cwt and 25cwts made a ton and allowance coal was never free.

The first Egstow Club was established in Stollard Street in October 1905, but when it closed in June 1911 a meeting was held at the Buck Hotel, on 5 July, to form a new club called the Coronation Club. Mr E. Tinkler was appointed president and Messrs Dan Hoult, Thomas Spencer and Mr Glazzard were elected vice-presidents. Messrs Herbert Clark, A. Beaumont and Sam Shooter agreed to become trustees. The following were elected as committee members: H. Wragg, J. Anchers, J. Griffin, F. Bacon, Thomas Mills, George Thompson, G. Rudkin, W. Bexton and J. Hoult.

The new Egstow Club on John Street was opened August 1911, by Col. G.M. Jackson who was presented with a gold key by the president J.H. Wilbraham. The club cost about £1,000 and 'every convenience is now provided and there is a large billiard room, a reading room, library, bathroom, smoke room and games room'. According to the notices in the window of this photograph, the club closed on the 12 November 1994 and the Egstow Family Club was set up.

Some of the stalwarts of the Holmgate Community Centre in 1957. In December 1952, the Holmgate Community Association tendered for one of the Nissen Huts put up for sale by the UDC when the POW camp was being cleared. This hut became the first Holmgate Community Centre and was opened by George Kenning in 1953. Around four years later in June 1957, planning permission was given for a new community centre, subject to it being built in brick.

The twenty-first anniversary of the Clay Cross Towns Women's Guild, 26 May 1967, in the Clay Cross Brotherhood Hall. Mrs M. Hatton, a founder member, cuts the cake. Looking on, from left to right: Mrs Fenner, Mrs A.M. Rice, the Mayoress of Chesterfield, Mrs E. Hill, Mrs E.M. Southerton, Mrs E. Whittingham and Mrs H. Spriggs.

The central committee of the Sheffield Equalized Independent Druids Friendly Society showing Mr John Renshaw of Clay Cross seated on the second row, fourth from the right. He was general president of this Order for two years in 1933 and 1934, and treasurer of the local Shakespeare Lodge for twenty-two years and an elected member of the UDC for many years.

The entrance to Kennings Park opened up in 1931. On the 1 July 1930 13½ acres of land adjacent to Holmgate Lane was formerly handed over to the UDC by George Kenning in memory of his father Frank Kenning. Its sole use was for a playing field for the rising generation of the town. 'It is now in the possession of the local rate payers to do with as they like so long as the children of the district are given free and unrestricted uses of the fields to play in.'

The large paddling pool in Kennings Park, which made an excellent skating rink in the winter. At the beginning of the twentieth century, many leading figures in the town were complaining that the children had nowhere to play, and that a recreation ground should be established. Eventually land was purchased in 1903, in the Broadleys and Bestwood Park, the purchase being funded by public subscription. However after a few years the repayments could not be met and the trustees had to sell the land.

The Dosher in Kennings Park was a purpose built swimming pool, fed by the Press Brook, which became very popular for dozens of people during the hot summer months. The money for the development of the site was a second gift in memory of George Kennings' mother and, 'there is no doubt that it will be called The Kenning Park out of compliment to the donor'. The Press Brook becomes the Smithy Brook at Clay Lane and was so named after the Smithy Bloomery—a sixteenth-century charcoal furnace, once in production on the Spoil Banks at Clay Lane.

Waterloo Street residents celebrating the 1935 Jubilee. From left to right, back row: Tommy Stevenson, George Ayres, Ernest Smith, Joe Stevenson, Doris Searston, Thomas Searston, Mr M. Searston, Ada Hartshorn, Elizabeth Stevenson, -?-, Geoffrey Stevenson. Middle row: Harriet Ayres, Ruth Ayres, Nelly Smith, Sarah Stevenson, Minnie Stevenson, Elizabeth Searston, Mrs E. Stevenson, Mrs B. Searston, Mrs E. Smith, Mrs R. Whileman. Front row: Louie Richmond, Iris Martin, Ernie Smith, -?-, Edwin Stevenson Mrs E. Bradshaw, -?-, Mavis Martin, Eric Smith.

Some Waterloo (Monkey Hollow) residents celebrating the Jubilee with a street party. The old No. 1 Pit Tip is in the background. The Red and Black Rake ironstone was also mined on this spot from around 1846, when the company decided to build two iron-furnaces. At the time of writing, this old landscape is about to disappear to make way for a new housing and shopping development.

The Fairground, c.1932, showing the 'Concrete Houses' just rising above the pit tip. This gathering marks the beginning of the August Feast Week, and in August 1932 the *Derbyshire Times* reported, 'The annual pilgrimage to the Clay Cross and Danesmoor Cenotaphs will take place on Sunday 14 August, The British Legion Service having now become a recognised part of the local Feast proceedings'. An officer to the left of the photograph can be seen taking the salute.

Jack Farnsworth of Thanet Street, The 'Human Spider', April 1929. He recommended this exercise as a cure for obesity! Jack was an all-round athlete and specialised in 'fancy gymnastics' and weightlifting. Here Jack is ready to climb up to the top of the gable-end by placing his hands on one wall and his feet on the other whilst maintaining a firm tension. This feat was performed between the Queens Pub and his home, which was a one-up and one-down.

Two

Chapel, Church and Whit Walks

The first New Connexion Methodist chapel in Clay Cross was built in 1824, being replaced by the one seen in this picture in 1848, in order to cater for the demands of an increasing industrial population. A Wesleyan chapel was also built in 1848 at the top of Holmgate and the following year a Primitive Methodist chapel was built on Bridge Street. Grundy's Free Methodist chapel was built on Thanet Street in 1857 and the Catholic church in 1862. At Danesmoor a New Connexion and Primitive Methodist chapel was built in 1869 to cater for the miners at the Parkhouse Colliery. At Danesmoor, Clay Cross and Tupton, the Church of England were well behind the Methodists in providing a place of worship for their new populations.

Clay Cross Whit Walk, 8 June 1965, with the Baptist Sunday school children on their float during the procession. Langwith Colliery Band and the Salvation Army Band headed the parade. At the service, envoy Mrs Grey (Salvation Army) led the prayers; Mr Muldoon (Reorganised Church of the Latter Day Saints) read the lesson, Mr Reg Rhodes, (Baptist church) conducted the singing, Revd W. Phillips (Church of England) gave the address, and Mr G.A. Fowkes (Methodist church) voiced thanks.

CLAY CROSS SCHOOLS.

Tuesday, June 3rd, 1868.

Scholar's
TEA TICKET.
Not Transferrable.

CLAY CROSS SCHOOLS,

TUESDAY, JUNE 7th, 1870.

SCHOLARS' TEA TICKET.

NOT TRANSFERABLE

Scholars' Whit Walk tea-tickets. In 1861, 1,100 scholars are recorded as participating in the procession, rising to 1,734 in 1867. With the opening of Morton and Danesmoor collieries, the number of attendants rose to 2,474 in 1868, peaking at 2,968 in 1872. The reverse of the 1868 ticket shows that it was made out to Sarah A. Ward.

Termination of the 1966 Whit Walk, in the infants' school yard, showing the rear of Shakespeare Yard to the right which was partially enclosed by iron railings. In the early days, the company's schoolmaster, Mr Stollard, planned the route and his staff meticulously checked and distributed the 'tea-tickets'. These tickets had a disciplinary and social control aspect and were only given on condition of regular attendance and good behaviour.

Opposite below: Another photograph of the 1965 Whit Walk arriving in the school yard. From the early 1860s the Whit Walk was organized from the Clay Cross Company's school with military precision, and up until 1882 the event was paid for by the company. The procession usually commenced at 'Clay Cross Hall', although there was a short departure from this when the company stopped funding the event and for a few years the parade assembled on the Bestwood Park area and the Holdsworth family from Alma House funded the event.

The 1966 procession passing through Grundy Road on to Broadleys, having passed through King Street which would be lined with its residents dressed in their Sunday best. In 1882, when the company's paternal grip was weakening, John Jackson (managing director) decided to stop funding the Walk and Teas and the *Derbyshire Courier* reported that, 'The public of Clay Cross for the first time are paying for the cost of the buns'.

The Sunday School Union leadership about to address the 1968 procession in the school yard. Alan Done is standing on the front of the platform, and behind him, from left to right: Reg Rhodes, Mr Fowkes, Mrs Grey (Salvation Army), -?-, Mr Stapels. Addressing the Sunday School Union in 1880, the CXC manager said 'as much good as Sunday School teachers were doing, there was one thing that they did not do and that was the reclaiming of the youths who had left Sunday School between the ages of fourteen and eighteen years'.

The Latter Day Saints proceeding down Kenning Street, June 1968. They were excluded from the Whit Walks until 1924, when they were accepted into the Sunday School Union: 'Moved, that we offer to the Latter Day Saints Church a hearty welcome to the Sunday School Union'.Rosemary Morris and Susan Stapels are holding the leading ropess and Barry Fox and Bill Lievers, (an ex-Manchester City footballer), are holding the banner poles.

The New Connextion Methodists leading the 1968 procession down Kenning Street, followed by the congregation of St Bartholomews church and accompanied by Lez Ball of the St Johns Ambulance. Amongst other 'walkers' are Sheilagh Done, Alan Done, Mrs Mills, Cliff Cresswell, Mary Staley and Pat Wilde.

Whitwalk, 1967, with four Baptist stalwarts who contributed much to the Sunday School, and throughout their lives helped to raise enough money to keep the chapel going, year-in and year-out. They always turned out for the Whit Walk immaculately attired. They also cleaned, scrubbed and prepared the chapel for any and every occasion—they were the salt of the earth! From left to right: Mrs Orill, -?-, Mrs Martin, Mrs Rhodes.

Col. Jackson opening the new Salvation Army premises, 12 June 1965, assisted by Brig. C. Renwick, from international headquarters. 'It is not often these days that a religious body outgrows its accommodation but this was the position that the Salvation Army Corps at Clay Cross found itself in, so officials began looking for more suitable premises'. The building cost £1,600—the national headquarters gave £250, the international headquarters £250, the old building was sold for £275, and Clay Cross Corps raised £520. This left just £291 to be raised.

Eustace Tinkler, master builder, with his workers displaying the 'cock' from St Bartholomews church at Clay Cross. Tinkler was a native of Bottesford in Lincolnshire and he served his time with Grantham's firm. Then, when he came to Clay Cross, he went into partnership with John Cutts. He resided at Belvoir Cottage, Thanet Street. His first big contract was the building of the cemetery in 1878. On his retirement, the business was taken over by Mr Fletcher of Clay Cross.

The Clay Cross church was consecrated in 1851, and the spire added in 1856, but the bells was not incorporated until August 1874–'The bells were ordered and arrived this week from Messrs Warren and Sarrs, London. The Lord Bishop of the Diocese has announced to preach at the opening of the bells (five in number) on 12 August'. In December 1936, the CXC gave £25 to the church for the restoration of the bells. This card was posted 14 July 1905 at Whittington.

In September 1944, a request was made by the parish church to the UDC to put a clock in the church tower and to provide two additional bells in order to make a complete peal, which was agreed unanimously. In April 1894, the CXC donated £20 towards the cost of a new organ.

On the 3 October 1877, it was unanimously resolved that a new burial ground be provided. The churchyard was closed for burials on the 31 March 1879, except for internment in the vaults. On the 10 March 1879, permission was granted and a licence given to bury the dead according to the rites of the established Church of England. The cemetery was officially consecrated on 14 June 1879. George Marshall was appointed Sexton on 9 December 1878 at a weekly salary of 24s.

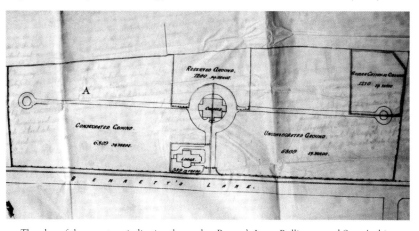

The plan of the cemetery, indicating the road as Bennet's Lane. Rollinsons and Son, Architect and Surveyor of Chesterfield, prepared the plans and specification for the erection of the cemetery lodge, chapels and fences. The estimate of £2,155 from Eustace Tinkler and William Mycroft, builders of Clay Cross was accepted. A capital loan of £63,000 was obtained from the Public Works Loan Board. The division of the burial ground, allocation of land and position was vigorously debated by the members of the Burial Board.

A view looking up King Street in 1953, showing the Salvation Army barracks which are situated on the left at the top of the street with the gable-end mounted with a cross. The chapel occupied the top floor only, with an off-licence, bottle store and garage occupying the ground floor.

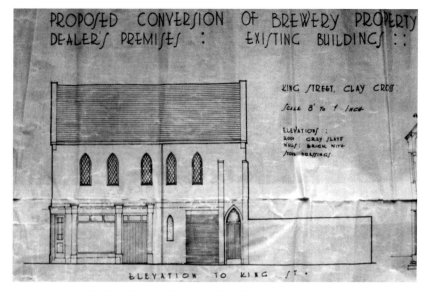

A side elevation of the Salvation Army barracks in King Street for the proposed conversion of brewery property into a motorcycle dealers for Mr Fred Barlow.

Clay Cross junior school netball team, 1954. From left to right, back row: Mrs Dorothy Young (Tilley), Mr Hardwick. Middle row: Margaret Dalley, Dorinda Thompson, Doris Knapper, Shelia Scothern, Mary Hughes, Gywenth Harris, Elain Martin, Brenda Clark. Front row: Cheryl Baugh, Ann Bacon, Margaret Walker, Margaret Walker, S. Cupit.

Clay Cross junior school athletics team, 1954, with headmaster Mr Hardwick. From left to right, back row: Margaret Elliot, Margaret Dalley, Hazel Knapper, M. Scott, D. Whittle, Diane Bowman, P. Smith, G. Harris. Seated: Brenda Clark, Margaret Walker, Jean Parker, Gwyneth Allen, Doris Knapper.

Clay Cross junior school, 1954. From left to right, back row: Dorothy Young, Frank Holmes, Gordon Bunting, John Pazloski, Graham Martin. Third row: Harry Lander, Alan Bates, Richard Finch, Wendy Womersley, Pamela Bright, Maureen Walker, Valerie Cox, Shirley Holmes, -?-, Roy Smith, Ivor Bradbury, Melvyn Haston. Second row: Elaine Martin, Susan Fox, Glenys Wilson,

Audry Allen, Maureen Kelly, Eileen Dunn, Sandra Holmes, Valerie Parker, Gwen Herdman, Angela Gardner, Joy Freeman, Sandra Harris, Kathleen Martin. Front row: Derek Wilson, Trevor Smith, Steven Collins, Richard Mullis, Wilfred Palfryman, Stuart Shimwell, Graham Ayres, Roger Boyd, Kenneth Slater, Melvin Plowman.

Clay Cross junior school athletics team, 1956. From left to right, back row: Dorothy Young (Tilley), Sandra Magee, Joyce Durose, Shelia Scothern, Mr Hardwick. Seated: Gywenth Harris, Margaret Noon, Janet Holmes, Cheryl Baugh.

Clay Cross Junior, second netball team, 1953/54 season. From left to right, back row: Veronica Finch, Dorothy Young (Tilly), Mrs Teacher, Margaret Collier. Front row: Gloria Chapman, Doreen Slater, Marlene Scott, Margaret Walker, Margaret Crofts.

Three

Football, Soccer and Nudder

The Clay Cross Zingari was established in 1900, when they signed up with the East Derbyshire FA in August, and were placed in division two of the Chesterfield Minor League. This photograph shows them displaying the Bayley Cup and Chesterfield Benevolent Cup which they won during the 1904/05 season. The Zigs were the premier team in the town but when the new Clay Cross Works team threatened their status in 1906, their chairman said, 'no doubt that the Works Club were strong financially and had an influential lot of gentlemen on their executive, especially when the whole of the foremen and underviewers were elected *en bloc* as vice-presidents, for who could sign players on better than these latter gentlemen coming into contact with these players every day as they did'. After a statement by Col. G.M. Jackson, the works' president, it was requested that at least fifty guarantors and the 'latter gentlemen' besides senior management, were expected to donate a sovereign each.

Clay Cross Town Football Club with the Derbyshire Cup they won in 1910, after beating Tupton Ivanoe 2-1. The town football club was established from the Sharley Park Club in 1880, but was wound up in January 1896. 'From the very moment our club went to the Angel (November 1894) it went from bad to worse and ultimately in the first month of 1896, had to be broken up'. It was re-established again in September 1909, when the Works and Zingari clubs amalgamated and participated in the Notts and Derby League.

Clay Cross Tradesmen Football Club in the 1904/05 season. In 1893, we learn that this team was christened 'The Liptons' after the famous sausage, and 'grocers and butchers are the chief constituents of the team and the matches are giving the strikers no cause to regret seeing their abilities. Indeed, the cheering was deafening, and such laughing was provoked throughout the game. Butcher Thrupp, butcher Longmate and Cherry gave a very creditable display. Jigger and Cox and Forester the publicans showing they were not daft, which in fact the Stretton footballers have learned to know'.

Clay Cross Red Rose FC was established in 1904, by Mr Timmy Binsley. This photograph was taken by Albert Heath at the end of the 1909/10 season and is believed to be the team that first won the Derbyshire Medals for the town. At this date the Angel Inn Pub was their headquarters. The winning team at this date comprised of G. Griffiths (captain), T. Binsley (secretary), G. Buckland, J. Barker, E. Holbrook, G. Smith, F. Woodall, S. Smith, G. Green, J. Bowen and Herbert Bostock.

Another Albert Heath photograph of the Red Rose team and officials for the 1911/12 season. Included in the photograph are: H. Smith (trainer), E. Bramley, F. Shaw, J. Parker, ? Whylde, S. Steeples, G. Whylde, A. Webster, W. Dilkes, ? Wisehall, F. Woodhall, ? Jarvis, S. Smith, J. Barker and J. Findley.

The Clay Cross Baptist Football Club was established in October 1909, when the Revd J.R. Cooper held a meeting for the young men attending the Baptist church. Mr Hopkin's offer of a field on the Tupton road was accepted and the following officials were elected: Revd J.R. Cooper (president); R.B. Bennett (secretary); A. Maycock (assistant secretary); W.H. Longmate (treasurer); W. Harris (captain) and W.H. Priest (vice-captain).

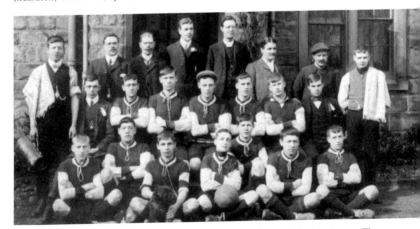

Clay Cross Parish Church Football Club, 1909/10 season, taken outside the vicarage. The team played on the adjoining Glebe Field and their headquarters were in the Parochial School Rooms. From left to right, back row: W. Holland, J. Titterton, F. Marshall, V. Harrison, Revd J. Blake, F. May, W. Phillips, F. Wragg. Middle row: A. Lapper, L. Swift, H. Birdin, W. Hodgkinson (captain), H. Orme, J.W. Nuttall, L. Clegg. Front row: E. Orme, W. Allen, E. Walton, J. Hankinson, A. Farnsworth, E. Holland, T. Hankinson (secretary).

Clay Cross Gospel Mission, winners of the Sunday School League for the 1910/11 season. In the leagues very first season, 1909/10, there were sixteen teams including CX church, CX Baptist, Danesmoor United Methodist (UM), Gospel Mission, Danesmoor Primitive Methodist (PM), Holmewood Wesley, Lings Row PM, New Tupton PM, Parkhouse Green, Stonebroom PM, North Wingfield church, Grassmoor PM, Clay Cross Wesley, Pilsley PM, Pilsley UM.

Clay Cross Wesleyan FC at the beginning of the 1910/11 Sunday League season. This was a disastrous season for the team when they lost eighteen matches, drew three and won only two out of twenty-three games. The Sunday School League was established to counter the growth of pub teams that were proliferating in the north Derbyshire coalfield, but they all kept the Sabbath and played on a Saturday with the exception of the tradesmen who played on Wednesday.

The Rose and Crown were the runners up in the Derbyshire Medals for the 1910/11 season, losing 1–0 to Hasland Red Rose. The championship title was taken away from them when the league was informed that they had been playing with an illegal player and were deducted six points. Apparently they had played J. Walvin, a professional, in several league games and their local rivals, the Red Rose, reported it to the League.

Clay Cross Rose and Crown, 1913/14 season. 'Since their connection with league football four years ago, Clay Cross Rose and Crown have never failed to win a set of medals each year and the ensuing year looked like being no exception. Holmgate Road ground will be again the scene of their struggles and the colours remain the same. Last year the club won the Derbyshire Medals, were runners up in the league and reached the semi-final of the junior cup'.

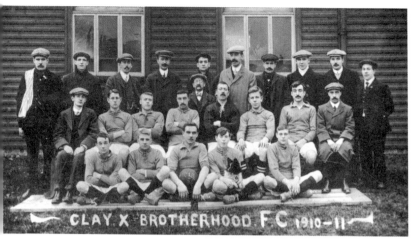

Clay Cross Brotherhood Football Club participated in the Clay Cross and District League for the 1910/11 season. From left to right, back row: William Large, John Whetton, Will Mitchell, E.A. Evans (hon. sec of Institute), T. Skelding, M.T. Mycroft (timber merchant), Jas Pettit, William Brailsford, J.H. Goodhall, Jim Calladine. Middle row: Tommy Bower, Jack Pettit, Jim Hawkins, Mat Pugh, Issac Hatton, John Macey, Ernest Anthony, Jack Morris, E. Pugh. Front row: Charlie Coleman, Jos Brown, Jas Brailsford, Jim Yates, Ernest Jaques.

This photograph appears to be the Red Rose team with their trophies outside the Angel Inn. The plaque on the wall reads, 'Henry Wragg licensed to sell Beer, Ale, Wines and Spirits'. Seen here is George Findley, standing fifth from left, and the second person sitting on the left is Mr Tom Palfreyman, whose family made a phenomenal contribution to Clay Cross Football for over one hundred years.

The Red Rose team, 1931, outside their new headquarters at the Queens Head Pub in Thanet Street. One of the teams best-known players was their left winger George Findlay, nicknamed 'The Flying Finner' who is seated second from the right. This team won the Chesterfield and District League Cup in 1931 when this photograph was taken. On the day of his marriage, George played against Unstone United and scored a hat-trick in a 7–3 win.

The Danesmoor Welfare Football Club. This club was established in August 1925, and affiliated with the Chesterfield and District League in the Graham Division where they finished fourth in their first season. Fourteen players signed on for their first season—Featherstone (goalie), Brailsford (captain), Shelton, Stone, Turvey, Wainwright, Worthy, Spencer, Cook, Jones, Palfryman, Evans, Hawkins, and Anthony.

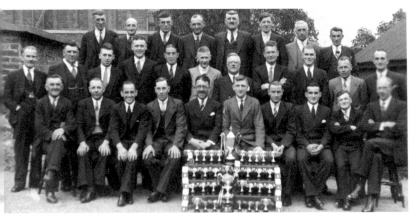

Clay Cross Works Football Club showing some players and committee members with the 1937/38 Chesterfield and District league trophy and the Graham Cup. This photograph was taken behind the Royal Volunteer Pub in Market Street with Col. H. Jackson and David Smith (insurance man) the Works captain, seated immediately behind the trophy.

The wives and girlfriends of the above players and committee taken on the same spot. When the Works team was first established Col. G.M. Jackson said he 'should be very pleased to assist all he could and to make arrangements for the team to play on Sharley Park—if it was carried out on proper lines, viz with pleasantness between the competing teams, and without jeering from the crowd when anything did not exactly please them.'

The Parkhouse Colliery Football Club was formed in October 1940 and took over the fixtures of the Danesmoor Welfare team in the Chesterfield and District League who had disbanded. Their opening match was with Eckington St Peters. The officials were Brig.-Gen. Jackson (president), A. McNeish (vice-president), J.T. Davis (chairman), Mr P. Smith, G. Dalley (treasurer), L. Slater (secretary and assistant secretary), W.L. Spencer. Committee members were: G. Brailsford, B. Bowman, S. Burdett, H. Bowler, J. Holmes, S Holmes, V. Harris, J. Palfryman, B. Slater and J.L. Williams.

Parkhouse Football Club, 1949/50 season, with the Central Alliance Knockout Cup and the Derbyshire Divisional Cup. From left to right, back row: E. Woodhead, M. Carlin. Middle row: J. Sims, J. Ashmore, R. Allsop, H. Parker, T. Lunn, T. Holmes. Front row: R. Beresford, F. Stone, S. Baker (captain), G. Dooley, H. Wragg.

Four

Tennis, Bowls and Cricket

Clay Cross Brotherhood Voluntary Workers (YMCA), known as the Pepper Gang, making the tennis courts and bowling green in 1910. From left to right, back row: Syd Hopkins (manager of the Kino Hall), M.T. Mycroft, (timber merchant), Harold Cherry (former manager of the Chesterfield Hippodrome), William Clarke. Seated: Jack Grainger, George Toplis, Edwin Priestnall, Arthur Atterbury, (killed in France), John Lowe (caretaker). On the grass: Charles Coleman, Issac Hatton ('a little but great man'), W.H. Cherry (local butcher).

The first sod of the Institute was cut Wednesday 17 November, with the opening fixed for 23 December 1908. 'It will contain a billiard room for two full-sized tables, reading room and small library, bagatelle room and temperance bar together with an assembly hall. The cost of the building was estimated at £650 and the committee planned to raise the money by £150 in subscriptions and a £300 interest-free loan. At this date the institute had a membership of 365. This card was posted from Clay Cross to Coventry, 31 May 1915.

The 'Press Gang' at the opening of the Brotherhood tennis courts in 1911. The group at the front of the photograph, from left to right: John Huish, *Derbyshire Times*; W.J. Mitchell, press photographer; William Armatage, *Derbyshire Courier* and Joseph Spriggs, *Clay Cross Chronicle*. This particular postcard was sent by W.J. Mitchell to the *Derbyshire Times* in 1935 and published in their 17 May issue.

The influential and middle-class members of the Brotherhood, June 1911, at the opening of 'their' new tennis courts. From a close scrutiny of some of their names, not many miners participated in this particular game either at this club or any other tennis club in the town.

The Clay Cross Cycling Club with their 'four wheeler', 1890. The original cycling club at Clay Cross was established in 1876, and was the second oldest in the country with its headquarters at the George and Dragon. By 1906 it had ceased to function and in June 1908 an attempt was made to resuscitate the club with medals being given for the best attendance. The president was Robert Cook, secretary H. Claytor and the committee comprised of G. Silkstone, T. Stoppard, J. Draycott, J. Clark and E. Fletcher.

Above: The Clay Cross Temperance Cycling Club around 1907–'For the past eighteen months there has been a cycle corps in connection with the local lodge of the Good Templars but at the last meeting of the corps it was thought advisable to make the club into a temperance cycling club and thus give a wider scope to outside cyclists'. Subscriptions were 1s per year and their headquarters was at the Wesleyan church.

*Left:*The CXC also established a cycle club in May 1897, but membership was restricted to employees. The officials were W.B. Jackson (president), John Parkin (secretary), John Steen (treasurer), A. Bramley (captain) and C. Brimlow (sub-captain). This photograph shows Billy Bowen in training behind the Bottom Long Row. At this date Richard Marshall was the main cycle dealer in the town.

John Edward Cupit, veteran motorcyclist of No. 238, Market Street, Clay Cross. He was one of the first motorcyclists in Derbyshire and still rode his motor bike when over eighty years of age. He had held a road licence since 1912. He was an inventor and constructed a model aeroplane in 1909, and was also an expert watch and clock repairer, as well as a poet. The Gaumont Cinema gave him a free ticket for life. He died March 1963, at the age of ninety-one.

Mr John Cupitt with his daughter on the second bike (R5843), his son in the middle, and his wife peering around their door in Market Street. The notice describes him as a watch and clock repairer.

Albion Cricket Club, Clay Cross.
Established March 17th
1853.

At a meeting of the members of the Clay Cross Reading Society, held in their Room, at Clay Cross, on Thursday Evening March 17th 1853, at 8 o'clock, for the purpose of establishing a Cricket Club, and forming Rules and Regulations for the same, It was moved by Mr Binns, and seconded by Mr Robinson That Mr C.S. Wilkinson take the Chair.

It was resolved That the Club be called "The Albion Cricket Club."

That there shall be a President, Treasurer and Secretary. — Such to be elected annually.

That Chas. Binns Esqr be President, Mr Robinson Treasurer, and Mr C.S. Wilkinson Secretary, for the ensuing year.

That there be two classes of members, Honorary, and Ordinary members, and that the annual subscription for each, be 5/ for the year. 2/6 to be paid at the commencement of the season, and the other on the 30th of June. —

That the ordinary members shall meet once a month, in the Reading Room of the Clay Cross Reading Society, and

At a meeting of the Reading Society in the old Stable School on 17 March 1853, the CXC were instrumental in re-establishing the Clay Cross Albion Cricket Club. The annual subscription for the year was 5s and members neglecting to attend the monthly meeting were fined 3d. It required two-thirds of the members to vote in a member and was somewhat elitist. Any member making use of abusive or improper language either at monthly meetings or on the cricket ground was subject to a forfeit of 6d.

Clay Cross Works Cricket Club, taken by Albert Heath around 1904, on the High Flat cricket ground which was named after a field name in the 1841 tithe award. The playing captain, Samuel Orme is seated centre of front row. From left to right, back row: C.V. Bryan, W. Wayne, W.A.C. Fearn, J. Morrel, G.M. Jackson, Guy Jackson, K. Bryan, N. Wilbraham, J. Dooley. Front Row: E. Armstrong, E. Fox, S. Orme, J.F. Harris, N. Salway, H. Pepperday, H. Eslington.

Clay Cross Works Cricket Club with Brig. G.M. Jackson, seated centre, with the trophy outside the Danesmoor Miners Welfare, c.1930. The High Flat cricket ground was opened in 1874 by John Peter Jackson and Sharley Park was named after William Sharley, the Clay Cross manager's gardener—'William Sharley be requested to mow the grass and otherwise level and prepare the ground forthwith in front of Mr Binns, residence, which ground Mr Binns has kindly given up free of expenses for the use of the cricket club'.

The new cricket pavilion on the High Flat was opened on Wednesday, 23 May 1934, by Brig. G.M. Jackson, together with Frank Lee, an official of the DMA and John Spencer, compensation agent. The Brigadier said, 'He took no personal credit for the erection of the pavilion on Clay Cross Park, but gave it to the County Welfare Committee, who showed no favouritism but simply made grants in accordance with a scale laid down and each district having a basis according to the number who worked there'.

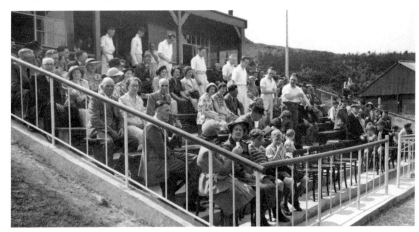

Col. H. Jackson's team, leaving the new pavilion to take the field against his brother's team. The Jackson family were well-known for their cricketing abilities and Capt. Guy Jackson captained the county side for nine seasons between 1922–1933. In 1924 and 1925 he played with the 'Gentlemen' and in 1927 was given the captaincy of the MCC that was to tour South Africa, but had to relinquish it because of ill health. He played regularly for the Sharley Park Club and in 1921 scored over 1,000 runs with an average of 60 runs per innings.

Col. H. Jackson's X1 and Capt. Guy. R. Jackson's XI nearly ready to commence playing for the Roland Jackson Cup in May 1952. This photograph, taken on the new works cricket ground, will no doubt rekindle many fond memories, but rather than name all the participants it will suffice to name just one—the legendary umpire Albert (Nanny) Wright. One batsman, protesting at Alberts's LBW decision received a short sharp rebuke 'Look int Greenun tonite youth'.

The presentation of the Roland Jackson Cup in May 1952. The cup was later played for by various works teams, extended to other local sides, and until recently was competed for annually. From left to right, back row: Mrs G.R. Jackson, Mrs H.H. Jackson, Mrs A.R. Parsons, Mr A.R. Parsons. Middle row: Mr W.H. Lee, Col. H.H. Jackson, Capt. G.R. Jackson. Front row: Miss Joan Jackson and Mr Roland Jackson presenting the cup to Mr Lez Taylor.

A group of sprinters about to get up to scratch on the Angel Inn Running Grounds around 1910. The four names on the back of the postcard perhaps indicate the participants—from left to right: J. Whetton, S. Burdett, J. Hawkins, ? Shirlock. Handicap foot races or pedestrianism have taken place on the Angel Field Running Grounds from the early 1860s, and were a big attraction during Wakes Week and 'Open to all England'.

Angel Inn Running Ground Committee, c.1910. Pedestrianism was a very popular sport in north-east Derbyshire and almost every mining community had a running ground, usually hired by a local publican who contributed handsomely to the stake money. These sprinters also teamed up with the pigeon fanciers and on race days they ran in with the pigeon 'wod' to place it in the master clock at the local pub.

A group of colliers in Waterloo Street posing with their 'snap dogs', c.1912. Rabbit coursing, which combined gambling with the cruel spectacle of the dogs chasing and killing rabbits in an open field, usually surrounded by spectators, was a very popular (although barbaric) sport in many north-east Derbyshire mining communities. Rabbiting, as well as being a popular sport, helped to supplement the colliers diet, particularly during short-time, strikes and lockouts etc.

Clay Cross Park Tennis Club was established in 1888, and held its annual balls in the company school lecture hall, and a glimpse at the guest list indicates middle-class domination, particularly in the company hierarchy with local traders and some professionals. At the fourth annual lawn tennis ball held in the company lecture hall, it was reported that 'over 100 ladies and gentlemen were present. Never on a similar occasion had the room been presented with such a pretty appearance, and a word of praise is due to Misses Howe for the excellent manner in which they superintended the decorations'.

In February 1908, we learn that the membership of the Clay Cross Park Tennis Club promises to be a big one and plans for a new pavilion were approved. A new club-house was procured the following year at a cost of £39–'The luxury of a new club house could not have been enjoyed but for the kindness and consideration of Col. Jackson, who interested himself in providing the necessary money and who has taken a deep interest in the welfare of the club.'

The new tennis club pavilion, opened by Mrs G.M. Jackson in August 1933. It was built by M.T. Mycroft with funds provided from the Derbyshire Miners Welfare Fund and designed by Wifred Fox, supervising architect of the Derbyshire Miners' Welfare Schemes. 'Little Miss Mary Pugh handed Mrs Jackson a bouquet of roses and was rewarded with a kiss'.

Clay Cross hockey team, outside the old wooden pavilion, May 1914. From left to right, back row: Miss Nutt, Mary Clayton, Ruth Clayton, D. Coulton, E. Crofts, R.F. Wheatley, D. Whiston. Front row: R. Holdsworth, W. Lamb, D. Bramley, E. Lamb. Peggy Jackson, daughter of Brig. G.M. Jackson, captained the Derbyshire Hockey Team for twelve years, and was appointed a member of All England Hockey Selection Committee in 1954.

The CXC's bowling green on John Street, 1956. Prior to this, the company had a green on Sharley Park which was part of the Miners' Welfare Scheme and was opened in September 1933. In July 1910, a bowling match was thus reported—'An interesting match was played at the Clay Cross Park Ground on Saturday between teams representing Clay Cross Park and Hepthorne Lane, this being the first match on the new green'. The Park Club remained unbeaten at home for twenty-four years.

The Rainbow Café, situated in the Butts at Ashover, was named after a play 'Where the Rainbow Ends' written by Clifford Mills and John Ramsey. It was built around April 1926 and opened for business on Whit Sunday, 23 May 1926. The cafe eventually closed in September 1939 but was used as a school during the Second World War for evacuee children who resided at Amber House in Kelstedge.

Rainbow Cafe was re-erected at Egstow and officially opened on 24 May 1952, by R.O. Jackson as the CXC Welfare and Sports Club. The contract for levelling and preparing the sports ground was awarded to Messrs Grimshaw Kinneare Ltd of Chesterfield. By October, the majority of employees agreed to contribute weekly subscriptions to the Sports Ground and Welfare Fund.

Five

Darts, Dominoes, Pigeons and Cabbages

Clay Cross Mid-Week Flying Club presentations at the Royal Volunteer, 1 October 1966, showing Eddie Shimwell presenting the Young Bird Average Cup to G. Dobson. From left to right: Dick Whitmore, Eddie Shimwell, J. Greenfield (secretary), G. Dobson, Joseph Peters (president). Average winners were R. Whitmore (combined), F. Boot (old birds), and Caunt and Dobson (young birds).

Queens Head Flying Club Presentations, made at the Shoulder and Mutton, Clay Cross on 29 October 1966. The prizes and awards were distributed by Dennis Skinner and he told those pigeon fanciers likely to be uprooted by the demolition of houses that the council would be considering their desires to retain connections with their sport. From left to right, back row: T. Cook, F. Mogford, W. Greatorex, E. Mather. Front row: Andy Martin, Stanley Martin, Tommy Churms, Alan Grassick.

Another Clay Cross Mid-Week Flying Club presentation on 13 November 1965, when a new cup, named the Kev-Glyn Cup was given to the club by the landlord D. Doughty. Eddie Shimwell is presenting a set of cutlery to F. Palethorpe who won the old birds averages. Looking on, from left to right: D. Doughty, W. Wells. R. Whitmore, J. Peters, J. Greenfield, Mrs Doughty. The club secretary reported a record year with a turnover of £525 and 972 pigeons basketed.

Joseph Peters taking his young birds to be picked for a training run (left), and Geoff Martin taking his clock in to be set at the Shoulder of Mutton club (right). Both men were coal miners all their working lives, proud trade union members, avid pigeon fanciers and allotment holders. The Martin family were members of the town's first Homing Society established at the Crown Inn in 1903.

The Pilsley and Danesmoor Miners Welfare Flying Club's annual prize distribution in October 1971. With a membership of 30 they held 18 races and dispatched a total of 2,808 birds at a cost of 4.88 d per head. The prize money per race was £16 and the pools and prizes amounted to £663. Mr A. Rawson, president of the Derbyshire Federation of Homing Societies, presented the various prizes.

Councillor Dennis Skinner (vice-president of NUM) presenting Norman Gill, captain of the George and Dragon Darts Team, with the Sheldon Cup, 23 August 1965, at the Royal Volunteer Inn at Clay Cross. The Dragon beat the Grouse Inn, Brampton, in the final. From left to right: W. Bexton, M. Bingham, Billy Hunt, L. Whitmore, Jim Ainsworth. Dennis also presented a cheque of £20 to the Clay Cross Derby and Joan which was raised during the competition. Mr David Daughty was the landlord of the Volunteer at this date.

Dennis Skinner MP presenting the Sheldon Darts Cup, 10 August 1971, to A. Gregory, captain of the Nags Head, Derby Road who beat the Star Inn, Pilsley. From left to right: George Pearson, Dennis Skinner, C. Gill, B. Wootton, D. More, A. Gregory, D. Moore. This competition held at the Volunteer Pub Clay Cross was one of its most successful and attracted over one hundred teams from Derbyshire and Yorkshire.

David Blakey, Chesterfield FC, presenting the Sheldon Darts Cup to Mr G. Else, captain of the Black Horse, Whittington Moor on 24 August 1967, at the Royal Volunteer, Clay Cross, who beat Blackwell Hotel by two legs to one. The highest score in the competition was 292, thrown by J. Kellet. David Blakey presented £50 to the Clay Cross Derby and Joan, which was raised during the various stages of the competition.

Clay Cross and District Darts and Dominoes league at the Shoulder and Mutton, Clay Cross 18 June 1965. This photograph shows the Red Lion Team, Clay Cross, with the Mr B. Shepperson holding the darts trophy—they were closely challenged by the Bestwood Club (2nd) and Shoulder of Mutton (3rd). Egstow Club won the dominoes with only a narrow margin over the Three Horse Shoes, Clay Cross, and the Midland Hotel, Hepthorn Lane. The Emerson Cup, for the combined darts and dominoes went to the White Hart.

Clay Cross and District Darts and Dominoes League presentations, 10 June 1971. From left to right, back row: Brian Garbutt, Freddy Vardy, Wilf Kerry. Front row: George Pearson, Ken Vaughen, -?-, Ronny Alien, Mick Scott.

Clay Cross Women's Darts and Dominoes League presentation, July 1971, at the Bestwood Workings Men's Club. Seen here is Harold Rhodes, former England fast bowler, making a presentation to Mrs J. Vaughen. Arthur Haslain, entertainment's secretary, opened the proceedings, Stan Sellars took over as compere, and arrangements for the function were made by Mr Fred Nicholson. The Darts League and C. Payne Trophy was won by the New Inn; Dominoes League and Green Cup by the Red Lion; Team Knockout Cup by Gate Inn; the individual darts champion was D. Palfreyman and dominoes champion was N. Bowen.

Cottage Gardening Society, Clay Cross

1852 June 3rd At a Meeting of the Committee appointed by the Reading Room Society for the purpose of preparing propositions for the improvement of Cottage Gardens, the following propositions were agreed to be submitted for the Society's consideration & approval at the Meeting to be held in the Society's Room June 10th 1852.

It was moved by Mr. Binns and seconded by Mr. Robinson.

That a subscription be raised and premiums given to the Cottagers having Gardens not belonging to the Company.

It was suggested by Mr. Binns that the Company should give £10.10.0 as the premiums to their own Cottagers, and subscribe £1. towards the general Fund, provided the Inhabitants of Clay Cross will subscribe £5.10.0 or £6.10.0 if possible.

It was proposed that the following premiums be given,

July 1st For the best cultivated Garden. 10/.
   "   For the second best. ———— 7/6.
   "   For the third best ———— 5/.
And that the above premiums be

The first page of the minutes of the Clay Cross Company's Cottage Garden Society. The society was re-established in June 1852, and a meeting was held in the Reading Room at the Old Stable School which was situated behind the George and Dragon Pub, down Clay Lane. The first Horticultural Society was established in 1845.

Clay Cross Company's vegetable and flower show, August 1967. This show was re-established in 1949, just after the nationalization of their collieries and the decline of the town's Horticultural Show. It was just over one hundred years since the CXC first introduced its Horticultral Society—'to encourage a spirit of improvement in the habits of the working-class by encouraging them to take pleasure in their homes and gardens in which to employ their time after working hours, instead of forming habits of intemperance'.

Holmgate Community Association Horticultral Society's chrysanthemum show, 18 November 1967. This competition attracted over 400 blooms and resulted in joint winners of the Mansfield Brewery Cup. From left to right: E. Spencer, J.D. Chapman, C. Slater, H. Chapman, M. Budarin. The Gardens Arms in Market Street were holding chrysanthemum shows from as early as 1859.

Six

Toll Gates, Carriers and Railway Stations

Joseph Sutton, Jnr, of Thanet Street, one of the several carriers plying between Clay Cross, Chesterfield and Mansfield around 1890. He succeeded his father, Job Sutton, of Cross Street, who died 7 January 1905, at the age of sixty-nine. Some other carriers recorded for Clay Cross were Jonathen Carter and Joseph Clarke, 1841; and Thomas Wilson, 1855, who died when his cart overturned on Tupton Hill in July 1855. He was succeeded by his son George Wilson, who also kept the Shakspeare Inn at Clay Cross. Samuel Rooth, another carrier in 1861, kept the Flying Dutchman on Thanet Street. Thomas Atkinson and Samuel Wilson, 1872 and 1881 respectively, also carried from Clay Cross to Chesterfield and Mansfield.

NOTICE is hereby GIVEN,

THAT the Truſtees of the Turnpike Road, leading from the White Stoop, near the North End of the Town of Derby, through the Towns of Duffield and Cheſterfield, in the County of Derby, to the Town of Sheffield, in the County of York, and from the ſaid Town of Duffield, to the Moot Hall in the Town of Wirkſworth, in the ſaid County of Derby, will meet at the Houſe of Mr. MASON, at Matlock Old Bath, on the 23d Day of October next, at Twelve o'Clock at Noon, in Order to conſult about erecting a Toll Gate acroſs a Part of the ſaid Road, leading from Derby to Cheſterfield, within the Quarter of Clay Lane or Woodthorpe, and alſo two Side Gates or Chains, one acroſs a certain Lane called Hen Mill Lane, & another acroſs the Lane leading down to Coney Green, and for other Purpoſes. Dated the 24th September, 1782.

Wm. EDWARDS, } Clerks
THO. INCE, }
RICH. SLATER, }

An advertisement from the *Derby Mercury*, September 1782, referring to a toll gate to be erected across the Derby to Chesterfield Road, the two side gates at Hen Mill Lane (Holmegate Road) and the lane leading to Coney Green. It would appear that the toll gate across the road at the top of Holmgate, Clay Cross, was erected sometime in 1786.

The Clay Cross toll gates on Stretton at Wynds Point were once situated roughly on the site where the Clay Cross post office now stands, and the gate straddled what is now the A61. In February 1876, the clerk to the Local Board of Health was instructed to write to Messrs Shipton and Hallwell pointing out the dangers arising from the toll gate post and requesting that they be removed as soon as possible. No action was taken, so the clerk then instructed Mr Smith of Crich to remove the turnpike posts within seven days.

Notice is hereby Given,

THAT the Tolls arising at the several Gates or Bars, erected upon the Turnpike Road leading from the White Stoop near the North End of the Town of Derby, through the Towns of Chesterfield and Duffield, in the County of Derby, to the Town of Sheffield in the County of York, called or known by the several Names of the Makeney Bar, Heage Bar, Higham Bar, Clay Cross Bar, Chesterfield Bar, Whittington Bar, Coal Aston Bar, and Healey Bar, will be LET for the Term of one Year, commencing on the first Day of June next, to the Best Bidders, at the Sign of the ANGEL INN in Chesterfield aforesaid, on the fourteenth Day of May next ensuing, between the Hours of twelve and four in the Afternoon, in the Manner directed by a certain Act of Parliament, passed in the the 13th Year of the Reign of his present Majesty, King George the third, " for regulating the Turnpike Roads;" which said Tolls produced the preceding Year, the several Sums under-mentioned, and will be put up at the several Sums so produced as aforesaid.

Makeney and Heage Bars,	£.230
Higham Bar,	149
Clay Cross Bar,	30
Chesterfield Bar,	183
Whittington, Coal Aston and Healey Bars,	577

Such Persons as shall happen to be the best Bidders, must at the same Time give Security with sufficient Sureties to the Satisfaction of the Trustees of the said Turnpike Road, for the Payment of the Rents agreed for, in such Proportions and at such Times as they shall direct. No letting unless two Bidders.

By order of the said Trustees,

SLATER and WALLER, *Clerks.*

CHESTERFIELD,
2d *April,* 1787.

Another advertisement from the *Derby Mercury* showing the first reference to the Clay Cross Bar being farmed out in April 1787.

Badger Lane toll gate at Woolley Moor was part of the Mansfield Tibshelf Turnpike Road, established in 1766 and incorporating the Fackley Gate, Badger Lane Gate, Tibshelf Gate and Dark Lane Gate. In March 1786, at the house of Samuel Wainwright (White Bear) in Stretton, these gates were let out for auction to the highest bidder. The previous year's tolls for the Badger Lane Gate fetched £46 11s ½ d.

Smithymoor toll gate on the Mansfield and Tibshelf Turnpike Road. On 6 May 1791, a meeting was held at the house of Samuel Hopewell in Mansfield for the purpose of carrying out an order made at the last meeting, 'for erecting a Toll Bar or Chain upon the said road, at or near a Place called Smithy Moor Bridge, in the Hamlet of Ford, in the County of Derby'. The order was signed by John Gladwin, clerk to the trustees of the said road.

View of Stretton, Ashover Light Railway.

Above: A view of Smithymoor toll gate looking down towards the Ashover Light Railway, Stretton Station which can be seen on the right almost opposite the main line station on the Midland Line and earlier referred to as the Smithymoor station. Timberfield House, the home of the Gratton family, can be seen in the top left of the picture.

Below: A Duffield to Sheffield turnpike road milestone post, situated on the Chesterfield Road near to the snooker centre in the Township of Woodthorpe. The Derbyshire Justices in 1709 ordered the surveyors to set up guide-posts at crossroads on the highways which usually took the form of a rectangular block of millstone grit indicating the names of the nearest market towns. Perhaps this order accounts for the base of the cross in Clay Cross churchyard which once stood at the top of Clay Lane.

Clay Cross railway station, built on the North Midland line, was opened on 11 May 1840. This lithograph of the station was done by S. Russel and published in 1842. The NMR minutes for 7 February 1839 read, 'Mr Stephenson be authorised to employ Mr Thompson in preparing the plans for the stations and executing the works at a salary of £400 per annum, during the period his services are required'. The seventy-two mile stretch from Derby to Leeds was officially opened on 30 July 1840.

In January 1866, the booking office at Clay Cross, which also served as a waiting room, was completely gutted by fire. This together with the increased traffic from the new Erewash Line convinced the Midland Railway company to build a new station complex at Clay Cross to service both lines, and this was completed in September 1870. At this date a goods-station was also opened at Coney Green on the Erewash Line and a branch line to Clay Cross Goods Depot was added in 1873.

A view of Clay Cross station, looking north, with remains of the No. 4 Pit Tip to the right. The 1841 census, records Samuel Ward as station officer, followed by John La Touche, 1844; John Gothard, 1844–1854; Robert Jeffery, 1860; Richard Eaton, 1864; J. Clarke, 1866; James Christmas Hays, 1868; John Butterworth, 1900; Henry Orchard, 1908; Herbert M. Reed, 1912, and A. Fearn, 1925.

Clay Cross Station from the lineside, taken by Edward W. May in 1966. This station was actually situated in Tupton and gave rise to numerous complaints throughout its history—'There is a deception about Clay Cross which irritates the stranger. You think that when you reach the railway station you are there—but you are not. It seem like a touch of fraud to find when you land at Clay Cross, that you are exactly two miles from Clay Cross and that your railway ticket entitles you to walk free of charge up the long hill to the town'.

Mr James Christmas Hays was stationmaster at Clay Cross from 1868 to September 1900. He was a member of the Manchester Unity of Oddfellows for fifty-seven years and was initiated at the 'Cheshire Cheese' public house in Belper whilst he was a porter at Ambergate in 1856. He was reputed to have never been 'on the club' or drawn any money out of his Friendly Society. During his time as stationmaster at Clay Cross he had seen three different stations. In February 1840, it was required by the NMR, 'that all porters and other subordinate servants of the company, whom may in future be appointed, be required to enter into the NMR Friendly Society'.

Two Midland Railway Company ambulance medals awarded to James Christmas Hays for first-aid rendered during his time at the Clay Cross Station. The medal on the left was awarded, 13 September 1900, for attending to Reuben Bannister who was seriously injured after being knocked down by a train. The other was awarded, 3 August 1897, for assisting an engine driver who had fallen from his engine and fractured his leg.

Retirement presentation to Fred Jackson, signalman at Clay Cross with Nobby Clark, stationmaster, and behind him Tom Marshall, station inspector, c.1962. The last stationmaster at Clay Cross was Mr Kimberly.

Clay Cross Station was closed on 31 December 1966, and a florist delivered a wreath with the message 'To Clay Cross Station opened by George Stephenson, gentleman and liberal. Closed by Barbra Castle, Labour, from Mr John Smith'. Colin Booth, a junior porter at the station commented, 'They just came with the wreath, said it was for the station and left it. So we hung it on the booking office door'. This photograph shows John Smith holding the wreath.

Another photograph of the closure of Clay Cross Station, 31 December 1966, with a group of railway enthusiasts protesting about the closure. From left to right: Jim Leverett, Bernard Bowdler, Dick ?, Hadyn Swales, Colin Booth. The last two porters at the station were Graham Whiston and Bernard Howdell.

A view of the Midland Railway Wagon Works, situated close to the station at Hepthorn Lane, with the No. 4 Pit (New Foundation Colliery) in the background dominated by the chimney and the distinctive tandem headgear. In March 1884, the Clay Cross Company sold off 2,000 of their wagons to the Midland Railway Company but later regretted this during boom periods when the railway company could not supply sufficient wagons.

A group photograph of the above wagon workers at Hepthorn Lane, c.1900. W.B.M. Jackson successfully introduced the Clay Cross Railway Bill into Parliament in 1902, and at the committee stage he criticised the Midland Railways' failure to supply sufficient wagons—they had been obliged to purchase 700 new wagons but they still suffered a deficiency. The object of the Bill was to link up the Clay Cross Works with the Lancashire and East Coast Railway.

The new Smithymoor or Stretton booking office opened in February 1884 after extensive renovations and was reported thus: 'An enjoyable evening was spent at Mr Barton's, North Midland Railway Inn, on Tuesday evening last, when an excellent dinner was provided for the workmen who had been working on the new station at Stretton. Mr A. Milner was unanimously voted to the chair, and Mr Bradley stationmaster, to the vice-chair'.

The Stretton Station, together with three railway cottages and two acres of land, came up for public auction in August 1967, at the Portland Hotel, and fetched £1,000. It was purchased by Claude Durham of Milltown Ashover. This photograph shows the rear of the booking office prior to renovation.

Stretton station with a view looking towards the southern tunnel entrance. In April 1840, it was reported: 'on Tuesday last, eleven new local stations: Duffield, Smithymoor (Stretton), Clay Cross, Staveley, Killarmarsh, Woodhouse Mill, Treeton, Kilnhurst, Wath and Royston were opened for the greater accommodation of the villages through which the line passes. Two trains each way stop at these stations'.

Stretton station platform, c.1920. The 1891 census records a small resident railway community at Smithymoor with David Nixon (signalman), Edmund Bradley (stationmaster), Gerstian Stevens (foreman platelayer), Matthew Daft (signalman), John Coates (wagon repairer), Aarron Davis (porter), George Barton (platelayer), and Emma Barton (innkeeper of the North Midland Railway Inn).

Stretton signal-box with stationmaster's house situated behind. Matthew Hunt was stationmaster there in 1848, Alfred Fewkes 1851, Charles Bird 1860, and Mr Harrison in 1872. Edmund Bradley came to Stretton in 1876 and remained there until September 1905, when he resigned owing to ill health. A presentation was made to him at the Stretton Mission church by Mrs Huish of Ford, who presented him with a Malacca cane walking stick and a purse of gold containing £62 5s.

Stretton ALR station, c.1938, which was situated almost opposite the Stretton Midland Station and where local trains to Derby and Sheffield were arranged in conjunction with some ALR timetables. The large sign reads 'Stretton. Change for LMS at S. Rly'.

Peggy stood on the Chesterfield Road embankment leading up to the Pirelle Bridge sometime in 1925. At the front of the engine is the driver Bill Banner, and Jack Grassick is standing on the footplate. The ALR manager, Capt. May is standing near centre with Capt. Guy Jackson on the carriage and the conductor Billy 'Picker' Allen is at the end of the train.

Bridget taking on water at Fallgate, 25 July, 1934, with fireman Bill Banner to the left and driver Harold Skinner on the right. John William Banner commenced work with the CXC in 1923, succeeded George Symonds as fireman in 1925 and was promoted to driver two years later. Harold Skinner started work on the ALR in 1926 and became fireman the following year, being promoted to driver in 1936.

View of Fallgate, Ashover Light Railway.

Fallgate station at Milltown. The ALR was divided up into five sections: Clay Cross and Hill Top Loop; Hill Top and Stretton Loop; Stretton and Hurst Lane Loop; Hurst Lane and Fallgate Loop and Fallgate and Ashover Loop. Bill Banner lived in one of the cottages opposite Fallgate Station.

TERMINUS OF ASHOVER LIGHT RAILWAY AT THE BUTTS, ASHOVER.

The publicity for this picturesque line reads, 'Ashover stands about 600ft above sea level, and is protected on the north and north-east by the Rattle and Fabric, about 980ft high. It is situated amidst the prettiest and most delightful scenery in the county, and is fast becoming a favourite inland resort with those seeking a quiet and peaceful holiday. The air is pure and bracing, the water supply excellent; two hydros and several well appointed old inns and a modern boarding house provide good accommodation to the visitor'.

From the beginning, the CXC used many internal steam engines which were all numbered. This photograph shows their 'Clay Cross C' No. 5 engine with a 12-ton wagon in tow. From the early 1950s they began to get rid of their steam locomotives and employed diesel engines. In November 1952, they purchased a diesel for the Crich Quarry and it was claimed, 'the manner in which it is hauling the quarry traffic is giving great satisfaction. Running costs of this diesel loco is considerably lower than the steam ones.'

Clay Cross Company's No. 8 engine inside the works, shunting up past the iron furnaces. Robert Stephenson supplied a good number of the early engines from his Newcastle works to the company in its formative years. In July 1953, the CXC purchased two Rushton and Hornby engines for £8,409, and, although this was the beginning of the demise of the steam engine at Clay Cross, they continued to use the steam cranes well into the 1970s.

One of the first Chesterfield Corporation buses used to run the ten mile journey between Clay Cross and Chesterfield. The bus crew are seen in uniformed white coats; the conductor with his money bag and ticket bell punch slung around his neck, stands outside the bus; the driver also in a white coat is seated inside the bus. The Corporations coat of arms are displayed on the side of the bus under the second double-window from the rear.

In June 1928, William Stoppard gave planning permission for the erection of a wooden garage, off the Chesterfield Road. The RA 3070, Dennis bus, on the right, was used on the Matlock run and the RA 7360 was used on the Ashover run. Both these services were taken over by the East Midland Bus Company. William had previously worked as a deputy at Parkhouse Pit until 1925.

Seven

Uniforms

On the 25 November 1860, a meeting was held at the Clay Cross Parochial Schools to inaugurate a company of the Rifle Volunteers. In February the following year the Clay Cross 17th Derbyshire Rifle Corps was formed and sanctioned under Act 44. Capt. Turbutt of Ogston Hall, the first CO of the Clay Cross Corps then swore in the first batch of officers, non-commissioned officers and 130 privates. The officers and non-commissioned officers were W. Milnes (Lt.), W. Clayton (Ensign), Revd J. Oldham (chaplain), W.J. Wilson (surgeon), William Howe (Col.-Sgt), Sgts George Brown, Benjamin Turner, J.P. Udall, and Cpls Robert Howe, Samuel Holdsworth and George Askew. The Clay Cross Volunteers were renown for their marksmanship and frequently won the inter-battalion competitions. This photograph shows some of their marksmen. From left to right, back row: Sgt Tissington. Cpl Brough, QMS Unwin, Cpl Butterworth, Sgt Vardy. Middle row: Sgt Neale (instructor), Sgt Milner (armourer), Cpl Brown, Cpl Claytor, Cpl Bryan, Sgt Fletcher. Front row: Col.-Sgt Wibraham, Sgt Brimlow, Lt George Howe, Maj. Wilkinson, Surgeon Lt Chawner, Bandmaster Sgt Sears, Sgt Whitworth.

The Clay Cross Band was sworn in on 25 January 1862, under the conductorship of John Hudson who was an ex-company schoolmaster who received the title of the 17th Derby Rifle Corps Band. Hudson was followed by Bandmasters Sears and Butterworth. The Volunteer Band played at the opening of the Co-op Market Hall in 1868. In 1874 they led the parade to inaugurate the new trade union banner of the South Yorkshire Miners Association.

In November 1907, the King inaugurated Mr Haldine's Territorial Army and invited the Lords-Lieutenant of the various counties to take control of the Citizenz Army. In March 1908, the Volunteer Movement throughout the country ceased to exist and was replaced by the New Territorial Force—'It is gratifying to learn that the recruiting of the New Territorial Force is proceeding briskly in the Clay Cross District and many of the old 'G' company have joined.

The Cyclist Company of 2nd Volunteer Battalion was established in March 1903, and the Battalion advertised in the *Clay Cross Chronicle* for recruits—'Application to join be made to Sgt Instructor, J. Perkins at the Armoury, Market Street, Clay Cross, or at the schools, on Tuesday or Thursday evenings at 7 p.m. By order, H. Oxley, Captain, commanding Cyclist Company.'

The Clay Cross Territorial 'G' Company of the 6th Battalion Notts and Derbys, marching to their camp site in the Peak District, led by Col. G.M. Jackson on horse back. Their first march out as a Territorial Company was in April 1908, when they marched to Ashover via Stretton, returning via Holmgate, headed by the Cyclist Bugle Band. The NCO's recorded on this march were Sgt-Maj. Perkins, Col.-Sgt Hoult and Sgts Butterworth, Farnsworth, Roberts, Matkin and Peach.

When the Volunteers 'passed away' in March 1908, there was no formal ceremony at Clay Cross. In December 1909, a new rifle range for the Territorials was built and the armoury was designated to the Populars (now Bestwood House), which is where Sgt-Maj. Perkins resided. The cost of the ammunition had to be defrayed out of Core funds and members had to purchase their own uniforms.

The Colours of the 6th Battalion, Sherwood Foresters, were presented to the Battalion by King Edward VII at Windsor on 19 June 1908, some fifteen months after the change from Volunteers to Territorials. On this parade, the Battalion was represented by Lt-Col. Jackson and twenty-three officers and men. The officers who received the King's Colours from Edward were the Kings' Col.-Lt Reginald Saxby and Regimental Lt-Col. G. Harold Heathcote.

On Tuesday, 8 June 1909, the *Clay Cross Chronicle* reported 'The ram, the mascot of the 6th Battalion of the Notts and Derbys Regiment, has duly arrived, and on Tuesday was put through his paces in the Peak at the head of the local Bugle Band. The mascot wondered, no doubt, what it was all about but improved in his marching towards the close of the lesson, and should prove a credit to his sponsors'.

Before the end of the nineteenth century, the Volunteers had long been considered inefficient, and according to Earl Roberts, in June 1904, the county force needed. 'Not a patching up, but a fundamental reorganization—V stands for volunteers who stay out late and drill now and then between seven and eight'. Col. Jackson at the annual dinner of the Volunteers in November 1907, said the change in Derbyshire would amount to the county converting some of its present infantry into artillery.

Above: On the 10 June 1904, Sgt Instructor Jos Perkins succeeded Sgt-Maj. Wells as Battalion Sgt-Maj. Perkins commenced his military career in 1879, and his first engagement was in Egypt under the command of Gen. Wolseley. In 1882, he received the Egyptian Medal and the Khediva Star. After cessation of hostilities he was drafted to India where he remained until 1892. Five years previously he had been promoted to Col.-Sgt, and on his return to England in 1892 he succeeded Sgt Green as the Instructor to Clay Cross Volunteers.

Left: Capt. Raleigh Hills, electrical engineer to the CXC, came to Clay Cross in 1901, to assist with the installation of electricity to the works. He was later responsible for the installation of the beacon in the Crich Stand Memorial. He died at Woodend, Cromford in May 1937, aged fifty-seven. On the 8 August 1914, when the 6th Battalion Colours were deposited in the Chesterfield parish church they were carried by Lt Raleigh Hills and Regimental Lt-Col. Darbyshire.

A CLAY CROSS COLLIER.
No. 109.

WINNING
HIS
BREAD.
Getting the
celebrated
"C.X.C.
Gold Medal"
Coal.
(See Nos.
107 & 111.)

SERVING
HIS
COUNTRY
The same
individual
as a
"Territorial."
(See Nos.
110 & 114.)

In 1907, the Clay Cross 2nd Volunteer Battalion secured the Clay Cross Town Hall (now the Clock Centre), on lease from the Clay Cross UDC, and converted it into a Drill Hall. They established a 'miniature' rifle club and used the hall for its range, but it was still hoped that the range on Stretton would be used again after modernization and the club would regain their proper position in the shooting world.

The annual camp for the Volunteers and Territorials was the highlight of their calendar and the very first camp attended was at Cannock Chase in 1873, under the command of John Peter Jackson (later managing director to the CXC) who succeeded Capt. Turbutt in 1866. Maj. John P. Jackson retired in 1891, being succeeded by Capt. Wilkinson, Capt. Howe and finally Lt G.M. Jackson.

Another camp photograph in the Peak District, c.1912. The tent squads consisted of one corporal and seven men, equipped with a bucket, one tub, eight plates, one kettle, one can, eight mugs and one clothes basket for bread. One of the camp 'hints' was to 'examine your socks and see that there are no darns in them to make blisters. If there are, wear them inside out.'

Col. G.M. Jackson, centre, started with the Battalion in April 1891, as a 2nd Lt of the Clay Cross Volunteer 'G' Company. He was gazetted Captain in January 1891 and promoted to Major in September 1900. He retired as the Battalion Commander in May 1912, attaining the rank of Colonel and was succeeded by Maj. Clayton. With the advent of the First World War he recommenced his duties and attained the honorary rank of Brigadier General.

On Wednesday 5 August 1914, the Clay Cross 'G' Company of the Territorials mobilised at the local Drill Hall for medical examination. The company was under the command of Lt Raleigh Hills and Lt H. Jackson with Dr Jackson acting as the medical officer. The following day they were given a 'most inspiring send off' and joined the other Companies at Chesterfield to be sent to the killing fields.

This *Dad's Army* photograph was taken by Albert Heath, c.1916, outside the Clay Cross Junior School. In February 1913, Col. G.M. Jackson, seconded by Mr Bramham, agreed that the Home Guards, under the command of Mr Wilbraham, should act in allegiance with the police and fire brigade, and take such steps necessary for the safe guarding of the town. They were also asked to consider what steps should be taken in consequence of zepplin air raids.

Stretton station, c.1915, looking north towards Chesterfield with the stationmaster Mr Angus and his staff, including two women porters who had been recruited during the War period as a consequence of the rush to the colours and the ensuing shortage of labour. Many women also worked in the company foundry, wagon works, brick yard and company farm.

Women Midland Railway workers, c.1918, at the Clay Cross station. Note the wooden construction of the station which had been altered little since its construction in 1878. The only person identified so far on this photograph is Nellie Wright who is standing on the right of the picture.

Branigan's Jazz Band on Flag Day, 1916. This event was arranged by the Clay Cross UDC on behalf of the wounded Russian soldiers. Cllr G.E. Wragg and T.W. Palfryman organized the event and hundreds of miniature flags were sold en route, when a parade was led through the main streets by the Ashover Brass Band and Branigan's Jazz Band. A sum of £40 was raised, which included contributions from Morton and Stonebroom.

Russian Flag Day at Clay Cross, 1916. In 1941, Winston Churchill established the Red Cross Russian Fund which was again organized by the Clay Cross UDC. The Bestwood Working Men's Club contributed much to this fund and George Kenning reported in April 1942, that the local fund had raised some £1,057, and that a balance sheet had been distributed to all subscribers.

The original Crich stand was erected as an observatory by the Hurt family in 1788, and was rebuilt in 1851 by Mr A. Linacre of Ambergate. By 1908, because of nearby quarrying, it had become dangerous and the CXC agreed to reconstruct it, but in 1922 they decided to donate £250 to the new memorial dedicated to those killed in the First World War. This amount was the estimated cost of rebuilding the old memorial.

THE SHERWOOD FORESTERS' WAR MEMORIAL - CRICH - NO.1
LONDON STORES
LANGWITH

Left: This Crich memorial was unveiled, 6 August 1923, and was dedicated to the memory of the 11,480 men of all ranks of the Sherwood Foresters of the Notts and Derby Regiment who gave their lives for King and Country in the First World War, and also to their comrades who so generously served in the 32 battalions of this regiment to the number of 140,000. Approximately £4,000 was subscribed to the memorial fund by public donation.

Opposite: The unveiling of the Clay Cross War Memorial was performed on Sunday, 10 December 1922. After a hymn and the First Lesson, an address was given by Brig. G.M. Jackson and after the Second Lesson, the memorial was unveiled by the Duke of Devonshire. After the last post was sounded, a volley by the firing party and a contribution from Robert Cook of the UDC, the Lord Bishop of Derby, dedicated the memorial. It was designed by Sir Reginald Blomfield RA.

The Danesmoor Memorial was unveiled on the 13 August 1922, by Capt. H.H. Jackson MC and the dedication was performed by the Revd W. Rowley. The cost of the Danesmoor Memorial and the unveiling was £385 15s 10½ d. This left a balance of 3s 8½ d and most of this money was collected through door-to-door collections.

This gun placed outside the old Territorial Drill Hall was a First World War trophy and was one of ten German guns captured at Canal du Nord by the 6th Battallion Sherwood Foresters, and was received at Clay Cross, 5 June 1920. Brig.-Gen. Jackson said 'It would be an everlasting memento to the achievements of 'G' Company, which had for so many years been associated with Clay Cross'.

The New Drill Hall, situated on Chesterfield Road, was opened in November 1938 by Brig.-Gen. Jackson. In 1935, there was much public protest about this 'everlasting memento' being dangerous after several children had been injured whilst playing on it, so the Clay Cross UDC decided that it should be removed. However, this did not happen until 1938 when it was placed in front of the New Drill Hall and then went for scrap towards the Second World War effort.

Clay Cross Brotherhood Ambulance Association, July 1936. This division was established in March 1932 and on its formation Brig.-Gen. Jackson was its first president. The divisional surgeon was Dr Alan Pooler; Superintendent Dr N.H. Pooler; secretary, J. Pawson; and treasurer F. Bailey. From left to right, back row: T. Whitworth, J. Williams, C. Marshall, S. Marriott, H. Tipping, W. Taylor, Cpl L. Ball, Sgt Holmes. Front row: E. Smith, J. Jarvis, F. Whiston, G. James, G. Guliver, W. Haslam.

The Clay Cross first-aid post with members of the ARP in 1939, outside the New Drill Hall on Chesterfield Road. From left to right, back row: M. White, J. Fox, J. Milner, H. Wright, W. Bowen, C. Calladine, G. Ramsdale. W. Brown, E. Milner. Front row: E.Q. Butterworth, L. Brunton, A. Anthony, E.M. Ball, Dr Glasgow, F. Baker, H. Carlin, P. Ling, M. Richmond, K. Rodgers.

In November 1907, Gen. Baden Powell's Scouting Scheme was announced—'The idea was that each young man should take six boys and train them in scouting, which taught them observation, life saving and a knowledge of their own country and their duties as good citizens.' On the 2 July, 1909, a company of boy scouts was formed at Clay Cross and Lt-Col. G.M. Jackson and Capt. Hilton took an active interest in the movement and placed the Territorial's Drill Hall at their disposal. Mr Jos Farnsworth, at the back of the photograph, was appointed Scoutmaster. 'It should be clearly pointed out, however, scouting is not as some seem to think, in any way connected to soldiery. It is a method of developing amongst boys the manliness and character that are so much needed amongst our future citizens. Scout craft includes the attributes of our best colonial frontiersmen such as resourcefulness, discipline, self reliance, unselfishness, physical activity and development, chivalry, loyalty and patriotism. These kindred qualities are taught entirely by means of practice and games which really attract and hold the boys. We think that we have written sufficient to show the utility of the movement. The motto of the Boy Scouts is 'be prepared' and the boys are educated up to this. Mr Joseph Farnsworth has been scoutmaster and he will be pleased to give information to any prospective member'.

A Clay Cross boys' brigade was established sometime in 1898 but appears to have lost out to the more popular boy scouts movement, but was then re-established on 16 July 1932. When the army and airforce cadets were formed in 1948, the membership of the Clay Cross Brigade declined and they stood down.

The 1st Clay Cross Guide Company was established on 17 March 1922, but a search of the *Derbyshire Times* has not revealed anything about its formation. This photograph was taken in 1925, which can be calculated by the yearly service stars appended to Nellie Wrights' uniform— back row third from left.

The 1st Clay Cross Guides on camp, in the 1930s, having their photo taken with a Brownie box camera. The only Guide identified so far, is Katie Rodgers—first left, middle row. From the establishment of the Clay Cross Guide Company they have had a long and distinguished connection with the Jackson family, with Miss Joan Jackson and Miss Peggy Jackson commencing as leaders and rising to area and county commissioners.

Mrs Bradley, ex-captain of the Clay Cross Guides, presenting Stephanie Hinchcliffe with her Queens Guides Badge; Miss S. Moore and Miss Ann Haslam, assistant county commissioner, are looking on. This award was presented at the parochial schools on 23 October, 1965, and was the 4th Queens Badge awarded to the 1st Clay Cross Guide Company in that year.

A group of Clay Cross Brownie Revels, June 1967, when around 150 brownies from Alfreton, Codnor Park, Riddings, Ashover, Auk Hucknall, Clay Cross, Morton, North Wingfield, Tupton, Scarcliffe, Shirebrook and Pleasely, attended the Clay Cross parochial schools for their Midsummer Magic. Mrs Kenning and Miss Peggy Jackson, Clay Cross division commissioner, judged the competition for the best pack sign.

Clay Cross Scouts and Guide spring fair, 5 May 1971. This event was opened by John Jackson, managing director of the CXC, and demonstrates the family's continuing involvement in the town since 1846, when his great-grandfather became a shareholder of the George Stephenson Company. At this date W.E. Cooper was Group Scout Leader, Mrs J. Whiffen, the 2nd Clay Cross Brownie Pack Leader and Mrs Sutton was 3rd Brownie Pack Leader.

The Clay Cross Town Band was established in 1908, after the Volunteer Band was disbanded when the Territorial Army was formed. The last Volunteer Battalion Band was the Clay Cross 'G' Company Band and the bandmaster was Sgt H. Butterworth. In April 1909, John Wardle, advertising in the *Clay Cross Chronicle* wrote, 'Wanted. A few players for the Clay Cross Town Band. Instruments and tuition free'.

A report in the *Derbyshire Times* for November 1921, reads: 'in days past the town was famous for its band, and an attempt is being made to regain its lost prestige. The new silver plated instruments, purchased by the Clay Cross Amalgamated Clubs, have been on view in the window of the Co-op during the week. The instruments have cost over £600 and will be used tomorrow when they will parade at North Wingfield church.'

In February 1892, the Clay Lane Local Board of Health decided to purchase a manual fire engine at a cost of £70. In March they adopted the rules and regulations of the Belper Brigade, and in August, fourteen applicants put their names forward to become members of the fire brigade. Ten men and two officers were selected. The uniforms were supplied by Messrs Morris and Sons of Manchester for a sum of £27.

By October 1892, the first official Clay Cross fire brigade was established. From left to right, back row: T. Beighton, James Stoppard, Francis Wright, Ernest Fletcher. Front row: Francis Aiken (Lt), John Unwin, John Chambers (Capt.), G. Griffin (foreman), T. Mycroft. Capt. Chambers was asked to resign because he was considered to be running an inefficient brigade that rarely practised any fire drill.

Right: James Stoppard, No 2 fireman of the Clay Cross Brigade. Commenting on fire brigade uniforms, Merryweather, the captain of the London fire brigade said, 'It cannot be said in the case of a fire brigade that appearance is unimportant. The general public cannot possibly be induced to support to an adequate extent, a number of ill-dressed, slip-shod individuals; whilst on the other hand they will contribute towards the maintenance of a brigade, the appearance of which is a credit to itself and consequently an honour to the town'.

Below: Advertisement, 1894.

TENDERS INVITED.

TENDERS.

THE CLAY CROSS LOCAL BOARD are prepared to receive TENDERS for the Erection and Completion of a FIRE ENGINE STATION, adjoining the Town Hall.

Also for the Erection of a PUBLIC URINAL in Market Street, Clay Cross.

The plans and specifications may be inspected at the offices of the above Board, on MONDAY, April 9th, from 2 to 4 p.m.

Sealed Tenders endorsed "Tender for Fire Engine Station," or "Tender for Public Urinal," to be delivered to me on or before WEDNESDAY, April 11th.

THOS. G. GRIFFIN (Assoc. San. Inst.),
Surveyor to the Board.

Clay Cross, April 4th, 1894.

In November 1923, a motor lorry attachment was coupled to the old horse-drawn fire engine 'in order to reach the fire more quickly'. In July 1939, a new trailer fire-pump was purchased because of the increasing threat of air raids. In 1949, the UDC sought planning permission for a fire station on the fairground in Market Street, but with the reorganization of the service on a county basis, plans were not approved for a new fire station until September 1952, and it was not built until 1954.

The Clay Cross part-time firemen fighting a barn fire at Coney Green farm, Clay Cross, on 9 January, 1967. Around 200 tons of hay and 150 tons of straw were destroyed at an estimated cost of £15,000. It was considered that the fire was caused by a spark from the exhaust of an old diesel binding engine.

Eight

Slag, Coal and Iron

A panoramic and busy view of the Clay Cross Company's Works, taken from the No. 1 Pit Tip. The offices can be seen to the left of the picture, next to the Midland railway line; and to the right are the foundries with the 'Big Wall' running up to the furnaces and then the 'Power House'. Situated just right of centre are the two wooden cooling towers and the huge slag tip that supplied the 'cracker' with raw material for years. The buildings on the right are part of Crabtree Meadow Farm, one of the initial purchases of the company in the 1840s, the land having previously been farmed since the eighteenth century.

A rare back view of the old blast furnaces, c.1900. This business card was posted 3 April 1906, at Chesterfield and was sent to Chas Ellis Esq., superintendent of the gas company at No. 42 King Street, Great Yarmouth. Gas coal was one of the main products of the CXC and they had large contracts with various municipal gas companies. This photograph was also taken by Albert Heath of Thanet Street.

The 'pig beds' at Clay Cross being made up with the previous smelt being gathered in front of the furnaces. The company were large pig-iron producers and in the early day used to mine their own ironstone along the ridge near the No. 1 Pit. The refuse from these can still be seen behind the Kwik Save. At one time there were about fourteen ironstone pits working along this ridge, but they ceased production in 1871 when it became cheaper to import ironstone from Northamptonshire.

A closer view of the 'Big Wall' that led up to storage bins for the raw material for the furnaces—limestone, coke and fluorspar etc. To the right of the Big Wall is the Turbo Power House where the company generated much electricity. In 1918 and 1923 they purchased two large generators of 1,000 KWs and 1,500 KWs and 'being desirous of supplying electric current locally invited the council (Clay Cross UDC) to give their moral support on the formation of a company for this purpose'.

Part of the stocking ground for the furnaces' raw materials that were transported up the 'Big Wall'. The 'Cracker' that broke up slag is situated to the right of the picture. In February 1878, the company were reminding surveyors of the highways and others that 'Broken Cinders can be obtained at the Clay Cross Works at the following prices—1s 6d per ton or one horse load, 2s 6d for two horse loads.' Charles Binns, the CXC manager was surveyor of the highways for Clay Lane township for fifteen years.

Above: After a feasibility study, the Bonds Main Colliery was purchased by the CXC in 1924. 'The opportunity of obtaining a proved coal field with shafts already sunk, seldom occurs, and its near proximity to Clay Cross is a great advantage to the Clay Cross Company. Coal fields in Nottingham and Derbyshire are practically unobtainable except in unproved cases and with say an outlay of three quarters of a million pounds'.

Below: Clay Cross No. 2 Pit, completed in 1850 and closed in 1934 during the depression. In July 1933, Dickenson, the manager, reported that 'the present summer is likely to be one of the worst on record' and in December preparations were being made to close the pit at a cost of £1,000–this would save the company £15,000 per annum. 'The repair and upkeep of the roofs and roads into the workings so far from the shaft adds materially to the overhead charges, making it no longer a proposition to continue as a separate pit'.

Morton No. 5 Pit, c.1937. In the early 1860s the Midland Railway commenced their Erewash extension line that extended from Pye Bridge via Morton and Danesmoor to the Clay Cross Station; the line was completed in 1863. In September 1863, the CXC were advertising for sinkers to sink two coal pits in the parish of Morton. By August 1865, the Morton Blackshale Pit reached a depth of 300ft.

Some out-buildings on the site of the No. 8 shaft in Flaxpiece. This particular shaft was sunk by the company in 1878, to improve ventilation and give easier access to work for some men at Clay Cross. It also acted as an emergency exit and was used to extricate the forty-five bodies killed in the 1882 disaster.

The Wingfield Manor Colliery, purchased by the CXC in 1924 for £5,000.

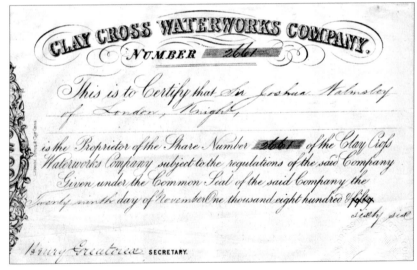

Clay Cross Water Works share certificate for Sir Joshua Walmsley, 1866. This company was established in 1856 when the Clay Cross Water Bill received Royal Assent and the amount of share capital was £6,000. The CXC took 25% of the shares and out of the seven Board of Directors, five were senior CXC officials. Charles Binns was elected chairman and William Howe vice-chairman. Howe assured the shareholders that 'their whole thoughts were devoted to their work and the best way of obtaining the full 10%'.

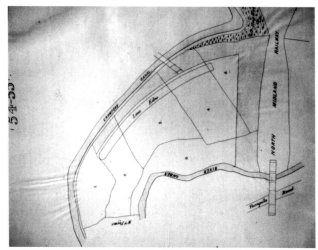

A plan of the lime works at Ambergate 1841, showing the kilns, canal, towpath, the River Amber and the turnpike road with the bridge to the right connecting the mineral railway (the Steep) with the lime kilns. There were twenty kilns operating in 1841.

The Steep at Crich was a one-in-four incline installed by James Campbell, the CXC's first resident engineer, in 1840. It was part of a complex that incorporated two self-acting inclines over three miles long, and connected the quarries with the lime kilns at Ambergate, (see *Clay Cross* and the *Clay Cross Company* for more detailed pictures of the quarry and kilns).

Stubbing Edge, the home of John Peter Jackson, managing director of the CXC from 1876–1899 when he took over from Charles Binns. He was the youngest son of Sir William Jackson of Birkenhead, who purchased the Hall and estate for his son in 1874. He was the first of the Jacksons to break with the Liberal Party and the rest of them soon enlisted with the Conservatives and have been ever since.

A family get-together on the front lawn at Clay Cross Hall, c.1920. Thomas Hughes Jackson is the gentleman with the white beard, to his immediate right is Mr R.O. Jackson, and to the far right Brig.-Gen. Jackson. The Jacksons did not move into this property until after the death of Charles Binns in 1887, when W.B.M. Jackson moved in until 1905, when he was succeeded by Brig.-Gen. G.M. Jackson.

The CXC celebrated their 125th anniversary on Tuesday, 28 August, 1962, when it held its 'Open Day' at the works. From left to right, standing: Mr G.C. Jackson, Miss M.B.M. Jackson, Ald. E.B. Robinson (Mayor of Chesterfield), Miss H.J.C. Jackson, Mr G.L. Jackson, Mrs G.R. Jackson, Miss R. Campion, Mr A.H.M. Jackson. Seated: Col. H.H. Jackson, Mrs H.H. Jackson, Capt. G.R. Jackson.

Col H.H. Jackson presenting suitably inscribed wrist-watches to four of the employees for their long and loyal service to the company. The Brig.-Gen. Jackson also had medals struck for a number of his employees and in 1925 his gardener was given one for long service. From left to right: Mr H.W. Padget, Mr S. Briddon, Mr W. Hall, Col. H.H. Jackson and Mr E. Dorricott who was representing his father-in-law Mr G.R. Walvin.

A training centre for moulders and core makers, sponsored jointly by the Clay Cross and the Bryan Donkin companies, which was established at Clay Cross in 1967. This picture shows the first awards to the 'best apprentices' in February 1968. From left to right: Peter Kirk (silver medal), Christopher Searston (gold medal), Roger Rutherford (bronze medal). Back row: Mr S. Farrer (managing director of Bryan Donkins), Col. H.H. Jackson (chairman), Mr J.D. Hullock (director).

The removal of part of the 'Big Tip' in April 1968, to make way for the industrial estate on Bridge Street. The tip was the result of about one hundred and twenty-five years of colliery and foundry refuse. This project led to the dislocation of many allotment holders and pigeon flyers, who were later found other plots in the area.

The commencement of the Big Tip from the works end, showing the overhead system. The train in the foreground is *Joan* on the reversing triangle, September 1930. Two buckets travelling on the overhead system can just be discerned above the funnel of the loco. This area was also a permanent adventure playground for the Egstow, John Street and Brasington Street children.

An iron pylon exposed by the earth remover in 1968. A number of these pylons were spaced at intervals to support the overhead system that conveyed the waste from the works. Tipping space was valuable and the main reason for the company purchasing the Wilson Estate at Coneygreen.

Another view of the Big Tips from the Chesterfield Road. This picture gives some idea about the tips' extent, stretching almost from the northern tunnel entrance to Clay Cross town centre and running parallel with Market Street. There were also a dozen or so ironstone pits on this stretch, mining the Black Rake and Red Rake ironstone.

John Street with the No. 1 Pit Tip looming at the end of the street. The houses on the left were built by the Clay Cross Company in 1900 and named after John Peter Jackson, managing director from 1881–1899. The other company houses on the right were built sometime in the 1920s and rented to the 'gaffers'.

Nine

Gongs, Votes and Politicians

Clay Cross Parliamentary Division election for 1922. This was a three-cornered contest between Charlie Duncan, Labour (13,206 votes); F.C.G. Masterman, Liberal (5,994 votes) and T.T Broad, National Liberal (3,294 votes), giving a labour majority of 7,212. Charlie Duncan was born in Middlesborough in 1865, and had been an active trade unionist (ASE), being appointed to general secretary of the Workers Union in 1899. Later on he became one of the principle officers of the TGWU and first entered Parliament in 1906, as a member for Barrow-in-Furness and served both as Whip and secretary of the Parliamentary Labour Party.

Charlie Duncan with local labour party activists with their improved transport in Clay Cross Secondary school yard during the 1931 General Election. There was a total of 42,931 electors and the election produced a 74.6% turnout. with Duncan obtaining 21,163 votes (64.6%) and J. Weinburg, Nationalist, 11,611 votes (35.4%). This gave Duncan a majority of 9,552 votes (29.2%).

A posed photo of Bridget Jackson surrounded by dairy and farm workers at Coney Green Farm, November 1936. Bridget was the youngest daughter of Gen. Jackson and stood as the Conservative Party candidate for the Clay Cross Division in 1935 and 1936. Arthur Holland won the 1935 election with 24,590 votes to Bridget's 8,391 votes—a labour majority of 16,199. At the 1936 by-election, Bridget stood against George Ridley and received 8,042 votes to Ridley's 24,290—a labour majority of 16,248.

George Ridley chatting to Mrs Lunn in the Long Row at Clay Cross, during the 1936 General Election. Active in the Labour Movement since he was sixteen, George was first employed as a railway clerk in Norfolk, attained a senior position in the Railway Clerks Association and served on its executive from 1909 until his death in 1944. He was elected chairman of the Labour Party for the years 1943-1944.

John Renshaw doing his rounds at Clay Cross. The miners at Parkhouse Colliery set him up with this horse and cart when the company blacklisted him and refused his nomination as a checkweighman, after he led a dispute that resulted in a fourteen weeks strike. When the men hit a fault and could not continue production, the company refused to pay them until they had 'found' the coal again. John was known to the press as the Stormy Petrel.

The old UDC offices, purchased in 1896 after they had relinquished their old local board offices in the Baptist school room. The UDC then moved into the Victoria Building in 1965, but later purchased back the old offices for the parish council offices, after local government reorganization in 1974. These particular offices, together with the fire-engine and depot, were seized by the courts when they refused to pay damages to a contractor in 1906.

The opening of the new Clay Cross UDC offices in the Victoria Buildings on the High Street, 5th July, 1965, by Dennis Skinner. On opening the offices, Dennis Skinner emphasised that 'it would be the public of Clay Cross who would be the openers of the new officers. If public service is presented properly the people would take an interest'. Dennis also noted that the building was very spacious with large cellars but he did not anticipate 'any Guy Fawkes activities, for the council allowed the public to come along and listen to their debates and to put forward questions and views'.

CLAY CROSS
Urban District Council Election,
1894.

Kindly mark your voting paper as below:--

Retired 1897

1	E ✓	BRAILSFORD.	97	445
2		BRAMHAM. ✓		130
3		CLARK.	-	358
4	E ✓	COLEMAN.	97 ✓	491
5	E	COOK.	96 ✓	394
6	E	DICKINSON.	96	596
7		ELLIOTT. ✓		298
8	E	FARNSWORTH.	98 -	525
9		GLOVER.	✓	230
10	E ✓	**GREATOREX.**	97 5/4	X
11		GRIFFIN.	-	190
12		HASLAM.		289
13	E	HOWE.	96 -	438
14	E	KENNING.	98 ✓	510
15		LESTER.	✓	147
16		ROWARTH.	✓	333
17		SHARDLOW.	-	291
18		SLACK.	-	261
19		TINKLER.		266
20		UDALL.		330
21	E	WOOD.	96 ✓	489
22		WOODHOUSE.		275

Printed and published by BALES & WILDE, Chesterfield and Clay Cross.

X To retire in 1896 Decr 79 - 6

A ballot sheet for the very first Clay Cross UDC election in 1894.

Clay Cross Division. General Election, 1935.

Polling: Thursday, 14th November.

The Election Address of

ALFRED HOLLAND.

Printed by Brayshaw & Bateman, Wheeldon Works, Chesterfield; and Published by
J. W. French, Election Agent, Clay Cross.

The central committee rooms for the 1894 election were in King Street, Clay Cross, and the election agent was J.W. French. 'In home affairs, Labour will carry out a bold policy of Socialist reconstruction. That policy includes schemes of public ownership and control in the national interest, of banking, coal and its products, transport, electricity, iron, steel and cotton'.

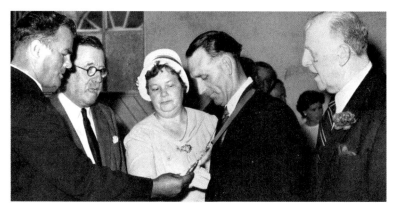

On 1 July 1961, Col. H. Jackson presented the Badge of Office to Cllr C.H. Holden, chairman of the Clay Cross UDC. On presenting the gong, Col. Jackson stated that 'he believed politics should not enter into local authorities, and to solve the problem of which coloured ribbon—red or blue—the decision was in favour of a maroon colour, giving each side an equal showing'. From left to right: Tom Swain (MP), Col. H.H. Jackson, Mrs C. Holden, Cllr C.H. Holden, Capt. G.R. Jackson.

From around the mid-1960s, the various chairpersons did not identify with the trappings of officialdom and refused to wear the UDC gong. When the UDC ceased to exist with local government reorganization in 1974, the medallion was donated to the British Labour History Museum and this photo shows the late Eileen Wholey presenting it to Terry Mcarthy, curator. It was later stolen from the museum and was never recovered.

Dennis Skinner, 17 June, 1967. In September 1963, Dennis was charged and found guilty of illegally using a hackney carriage to carry electors, or their proxies, to and from the poll. When seen by the police he was said to have replied, 'is this another Tory trick'. He was found guilty, fined £620 and ordered to pay £65 13s 6d expenses, and 12½ guineas advocates fee. However, he appealed against the verdict in November and won. The essence of the case was whether or not Dennis knew he was using a public service vehicle. The appeal court found that, 'after considerable heart-searching we are not sure that he did!'

Graham Smith, Charlie Bunting and Dennis Skinner, Labour Party and UDC members, attending Danesmoor Derby and Joan Christmas Party, December 1967. Mrs Murial Simpson, matron of the Clay Cross Residential Home, was presented with a bouquet of flowers and each member received £3 10s Christmas Box. The Clay Cross Labour Party were responsible, through their elected members, for the building of the new Derby and Joan centres in Clay Cross, Danesmoor and Holmgate during the 1960s.